PSYCHOMETRIC & IQ TESTS

Sample tests, questions, and help on how to prepare for and pass psychometric & IQ assessments.

www.How2Become.com

Orders: Please contact How2become Ltd, Suite 1, 60 Churchill Square Business Centre, Kings Hill, Kent ME19 4YU.

You can order through Amazon.co.uk under ISBN: 9781912370641, via the website www.How2Become.com or through Gardners.com.

ISBN: 9781912370641

First published in 2019 by How2Become Ltd.

Typeset for How2Become Ltd by Gemma Butler.

Disclaimer

Every effort has been made to ensure that the information contained within this guide is accurate at the time of publication. How2Become Ltd is not responsible for anyone failing any part of any selection process as a result of the information contained within this guide. How2Become Ltd and their authors cannot accept any responsibility for any errors or omissions within this guide, however caused. No responsibility for loss or damage occasioned by any person acting, or refraining from action, as a result of the material in this publication can be accepted by How2Become Ltd.

The information within this guide does not represent the views of any third party service or organisation.

Get FREE access to online tests at:

www.MyPsychometricTests.com

Get FREE access to online interview training at:

www.PassMyInterview.com

Contents

Introduction To Your Guide

Psychometric Tests are becoming increasingly popular during job selection processes, and test a variety of qualities and attributes. Psychometric testing is primarily used by employers to assess attributes such as numerical reasoning, verbal reasoning, and diagrammatic reasoning. Within this guide, we have provided you with many different testing sections, all of which form different parts of Psychometric assessment. This includes:

Numerical Reasoning. Numerical reasoning assesses your understanding of numbers, data, and the relationship between different numbers.

Verbal Reasoning. Verbal reasoning assesses your understanding of words, relationships between words, and the depth of your knowledge in relation to meanings, and grammatical basics.

Non-Verbal Reasoning. Non-Verbal reasoning is designed to test your understanding of shapes, and the relationships between different shapes in a sequence, or in the same pattern.

Spatial Reasoning. Spatial reasoning is designed to test the way you interpret images, and how well you can visualise movement or change between different images.

Mechanical Aptitude. Mechanical Aptitude tests your understanding of mechanics, and how forces interact with objects.

Personality Tests. Personality tests are used by employers to ascertain whether somebody is the right personal fit for their company.

Along with this, we've also included some IQ questions, which will test all of the above too. So, this book should prepare you for every single type of Psychometric Test that you might encounter, if you're being asked to take a pre-employment test.

In order to make the most of this book, take your time, and go through each section slowly and carefully. If you get an answer wrong, use our handy explanations to work out why you got the answer wrong, and then apply these tips to the next set of questions.

With our guidance, by the end of this book you will be perfectly placed to ace any Psychometric assessment that you encounter. So, without further ado, let's get testing!

The how2become team

The How2Become Team

Numerical Reasoning

A Numerical Reasoning Test is designed to assess mathematical knowledge through number-related assessments. These assessments can be of different difficulty levels, and will all vary depending on who you are sitting the test for. So, be sure to find out what type of Numerical Reasoning Test you will be sitting, to ensure you are fully able to practice prior to the assessment.

The majority of Numerical Reasoning Tests are administered to candidates who are applying for managerial, graduate or professional positions; any job that deals with making inferences in relation to statistical, financial or numerical data. However, some employers may use these tests as a way of determining important job-related skills such as time management and problem solving efficiency.

Numerical Reasoning Tests cover a wide range of mathematical formulas, and so it is imperative to comprehend the skills and knowledge required to work out the mathematics involved. Most Numerical Reasoning Tests contain questions in relation to:

Adding	Subtracting	Dividing	Multiplying
Fractions	Percentages	Decimals	Ratios
Charts and Graphs	Mean, Mode, Median, Range	Areas and Perimeters	Number Sequences
Time	Conversions	Measurements	Money
Proportions	Formulae	Data Interpretation	Quantitative Data
Data Analysis	Correlations	Statistics	Shapes

Your performance in a Numerical Reasoning Test can undoubtedly be bettered through practise! Getting to grips with the format of the test, and gaining an insight into the typical questions you are likely to face will only work to your advantage.

The more you practise, the more you will see your performance excel! With any psychometric test, it is important to fully maximise your skills and knowledge prior to your assessment to ensure the best result.

This comprehensive guide will provide you with lots of sample questions, similar to those that will be found on your Numerical Reasoning Test. Our insightful and ultimate preparation guide will allow you to grasp each question type, understand what is expected, and show you how to work out the correct answer.

Numerical Reasoning Tests vary in their format, in both types of question and difficulty. However, they all test similar arithmetic. Before taking your actual test, we advise that you research the type of test that you will be required to sit. The key components which distinguish different Numerical Reasoning Tests, are format and difficulty.

Formats:

- Graph and Charts – to interpret and analyse data and answer questions in relation to that data.

- Word Problems – short word problems or passages that deal with riddles and/or calculations.

- Number Sequences – the ability to find the pattern or correlation amongst a sequence.

- Basic Maths – demonstrate basic arithmetical understanding.

Level of Difficulty:

- Basic – simple mathematical formulas and calculations, interpretation, analysis.

- Intermediate – interpretation, equations, charts and graphs, statistics.

- Advanced – critical reasoning and analysis, quantitative reasoning.

Levels of difficulty and different formats are determined by the job for which you are applying. Your test will solely depend on the nature of the job and the position you are applying for, and therefore the requirements for each test and desired level of ability, will vary.

On the following pages you will find some helpful tips to refresh your maths knowledge.

+	Addition		$\propto$	Direct Proportion
−	Subtraction		$b \propto \frac{1}{m}$	Inverse Proportion
×	Multiplication		∞	Infinite
÷	Division		A^b	Indices
=	Equals		a^2	Squared
≠	Not Equal		a^3	Cubed
≈	Equals Approximately		a^5	To the Power 5
≡	Identical to		$\angle$	Angle
<	Less Than		$A \times 10^n$	Standard Form
≤	Less Than or Equal to		Σ	Sum Of
>	More Than		$\sqrt{}$	Square Root
≥	More Than or Equal to		$\sqrt[3]{}$	Cube Root
Ø	Null		$\cap$	Intersection
%	Percentage		$\cup$	Union
.	Decimal		π	Pi
a/b	Fraction		$°$	Degree
( )	Parenthesis (Brackets)		$\therefore$	Therefore
x	Unknown Variable		$\perp$	Perpendicular

TERM = A term is a single number, letter or product (multiplication) of numbers and letters.

- x x^2 $8x^3$

EXPRESSION = An expression is a short algebraic statement made up of one or more terms.

- $3x - 2$ $xy - x$

EQUATION = An equation is formed by setting two expressions to be equal to one another, by placing an equals sign between them.

$3x + 4 = 10$

Find x percent of y

To express a number (x), as a percentage of another number (y) you will need to divide x by y and then multiply by 100.

35% of 300

Step 1 = 300 ÷ 100 = 3

Step 2 = 3 × 35 = 105.

Step 3 = 105 is 35% of 300.

Alternatively, you can convert the percentage into a decimal. So 35% becomes 0.35 × 300 = 105.

Expressing x as a percent of y

To express a number as a percentage of something else, you will need to divide x by y and then multiply by 100.

Write 30 p as a percentage of £1.20

Step 1 = Convert the pounds into pence. You need to work with the same units.

Step 2 = Divide 30 p by 120 p.

When it comes to algebra, letters and/ or symbols can be used to represent numbers.

Step 3 = Multiply this by 100.
0.25 × 100 = 25%

BIDMAS

The order of operations is as follows:

Brackets ( )

Indices X^2

Division ÷

Multiplication ×   If division and multiplication are all that is left, work them out from left to right, in the order that they appear.

Addition +

Subtraction −   If addition and subtraction are all that is left, work them out from left to right, in the order that they appear.

Inputs and Outputs

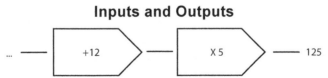

In order to work out the missing number at the start of the sequence, you will need to work backwards.

When working backwards, you need to do the OPPOSITE.

For example: 125 ÷ 5 − 12 = 13

You can factor '13' into the equation to confirm that you have the correct answer, and the equation works.

Speed, Distance, and Time

The below triangle shows the relationship between speed, distance and time.

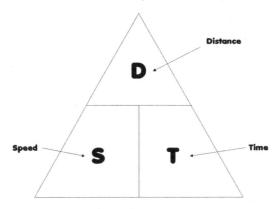

To work out the average **speed**, place your thumb over the speed variable ('S'), and then do the calculation.

- Speed = Distance ÷ Time

- 75 miles ÷ 1 hour 15 minutes (1.25) = 60 mph

To work out the **distance** travelled, place your thumb over the distance variable ('D'), and then work out the equation.

- Distance = Speed × Time

- 60 mph × 1 hour 15 minutes (1.25) = 75 miles

To work out the **time** taken, place your thumb over the time variable ('T'), and then work out the equation.

- Time = Distance ÷ Speed

- 75 miles ÷ 60 mph = 1.25 hours (1 hour 15 minutes)

Word Problems

Tackling word problems is relatively easy once you know the simple rule, and that rule is this: break up the problem, and pick out all of the key information you need in order to solve the maths problem.

A school has organised a school trip to London to see a show. In total there are 45 children and 9 adults attending. Work out the ratio of children to adults attending the trip. Give your answer in its simplest form.

As you can see, the above example is full of lots of information. Let's make this easier to understand:

~~A school has organised a school trip to London to see a show. In total there are~~ 45 children and 9 adults ~~attending~~. Work out the ratio of children to adults ~~attending the trip. Give your answer in its~~ simplest form.

Now we are left with the following information:

45 children

9 adults

Work out the ratio (in its simplest form).

= 45 : 9

This can be simplified to 5 : 1

Basic 1

Question 1. The average temperature throughout a 5-day period was 65 degrees. If the temperature was 67 degrees on two of the days, 70 degrees on another, and 68 degrees on another, what was it on the fifth day?

A	B	C	D	E
53	57	58	60	61

Question 2. If one box of pens costs £1.90, how much will 7 boxes cost if a customer has a 10% money off voucher?

A	B	C	D	E
£14.30	£11.97	£12.87	£13.30	£13.49

Question 3. 5 boxes of pencils cost a total of £12.00. If there are 20 pencils in each box, how much does one pencil cost?

A	B	C	D	E
£1.20	£0.03	£0.60	£0.12	£1.80

Question 4. If 3 boxes of pencils cost £4.56 in total, and 5 boxes of pens cost £1.12 each, how much will two boxes of pencils and 3 boxes of pens cost in total?

A	B	C	D	E
£13.68	£7.36	£6.36	£7.40	£6.40

Question 5. Julia wakes up at 6:40 am. It takes her 16 minutes to get ready for work, 12 minutes to eat her breakfast and 47 minutes to travel to work. What time does she arrive at work?

A	B	C	D	E
7:45 am	8:02 am	7:50 am	7:55 am	8:05 am

Question 6. A worker's toolbox weighs 22 lbs when it is full. He removes a hammer (1.7 lbs), a saw (1.50 lbs), a chisel (0.50 lbs), a torch (1.98 lbs) and a tape measure (0.25 lbs). How much does the toolbox weigh now?

A	B	C	D	E
16.07 lbs	15.17 lbs	15.07 lbs	16.17 lbs	17.27 lbs

Question 7. If there are 18 grams of fat in 100 grams of chocolate, how many grams of fat are there in 750 grams of chocolate?

A	B	C	D	E
126	135	18	700	74

Question 8. $\frac{3}{5}$ of a school's teachers receive manual handling training. If there are 85 teachers in total, how many of them have not received the training?

A	B	C	D	E
17	51	75	15	34

Question 9. It takes a swimmer 30 minutes to swim a mile. At what speed is she swimming?

A	B	C	D	E
2 mph	3 mph	5 mph	30 mph	60 mph

Question 10. If you spend £14.45 on a train ticket, £11.35 on your lunch, and £32.77 on a theatre ticket, how much do you have left from £100?

A	B	C	D	E
£43.14	£43.41	£41.43	£58.57	£35.83

Question 11. Mrs Martin wants to purchase a t-shirt, a pair of shoes, a dress, and a pair of jeans, which cost £11.97, £109.95, £12.95 and £22 respectively. How much change will she have from £195?

A	B	C	D	E
£38.13	£39.00	£48.13	£41.00	£46.57

Question 12. Mrs Fuller wants to return a t-shirt, a pair of designer shoes, a dress and a pair of jeans, which cost £12.95, £85.99, £17.99 and £22.99 respectively. How much does she stand to gain if all the items are returned?

A	B	C	D	E
£149.92	£133.92	£132.92	£139.91	£139.92

Question 13. A car is listed for sale at £17,500. The sales person then offers you a 5% discount. How much is the car reduced by?

A	B	C	D	E
£16, 625	£875	£900	£8,750	£925

Question 14. A man swims 69 lengths of a 25-metre pool. How far has he swum in total?

A	B	C	D	E
1,722 m	1,725 m	690 m	276 m	1,750 m

Question 15. A man swims 72 lengths of a 25-metre pool. If it takes him 40 seconds to swim one length, what time will he finish if he starts swimming at 2:05 pm?

A	B	C	D	E
3.17 am	2.30 pm	2.53 pm	3.17 pm	2.45 pm

Question 16. If a Police Officer's shoes last on average 24 weeks, how many pairs of shoes will she get through during an 18-year career?

A	B	C	D	E
36	39	40	42	44

Question 17. There are 55,000 people in a football stadium. If 22% are female, how many are male?

A	B	C	D	E
33,000	42,950	42,900	12,100	26,750

Question 18. If 60% of a hotel's bedrooms are occupied and the remaining 136 are not, how many rooms does the hotel have in total?

A	B	C	D	E
340	350	290	204	355

Question 19. If 70% of a hotel's bedrooms are occupied and the remaining 48 are not, how many rooms does the hotel have in total?

A	B	C	D	E
160	112	162	144	154

Question 20. A petrol tank holds 770 gallons of fuel. If it already contains 200 gallons of fuel, how much would it cost to fill up if it costs £4.12 per 5 gallons?

A	B	C	D	E
£114	£900	£560	£469.68	£782.13

Question 21. Gerard walks for 6 hours in total. During the first three hours he walks at a pace of 4 km/h. During the fourth hour he walks at a pace of 3.5 km/h and during the fifth and sixth hours he walks at a pace of 3 km/h. How much ground will he have covered after the 6 hours are complete?

A	B	C	D	E
20.5 km	21.5 km	22.5 km	23.5 km	24.5 km

Question 22. It takes Jessen 45 minutes to walk 3 miles to work. At what pace does he walk?

A	B	C	D	E
7 mph	4 mph	6 mph	5 mph	8 mph

Question 23. Jeremy spends 2 hours and 25 minutes on the phone talking to his friend abroad. If the call costs 9 pence per 5 minutes, how much does the call cost in total?

A	B	C	D	E
£3.61	£4.32	£2.61	£4.05	£3.78

Question 24. An office floor takes 240 tiles to cover. A man buys 18 boxes, each containing 6 tiles. How many more boxes does he need to complete the job?

A	B	C	D	E
132	22	4	8	10

Question 25. Charlie pays £97.70 per month on her council tax bill and, because she is single, she qualifies for a 25% discount. How much will she have paid after 3 years?

A	B	C	D	E
£2,637.90	£2,937.20	£879.30	£3,517.20	£3,845.65

Question 26. A worker is required to be at work for 8 hours a day. She is entitled to three 20-minute breaks and one 1-hour lunch break during that 8-hour period. If she works for 5 days per week, how many hours will she have worked after 7 weeks?

A	B	C	D	E
225	294	280	140	210

Q27. What is the value of x?

$3x - 115 = 875$

A	B	C	D	E
763	330	560	345	485

Question 28. What is the value of x?

$$\frac{5x - 15}{5} = 8$$

A	B	C	D	E
12	5	10	11	8

Question 29. What is the value of x?

$$\frac{9x - 122}{4} = 10$$

A	B	C	D	E
18	36	19	82	65

Question 30. What is the value of x?

$$\frac{7x - 5}{4} = 11$$

A	B	C	D	E
11	7	5	10	9

Answers to Basic 1

Q1. A = 53

$65 \times 5 = 325$

$325 - (67 + 67 + 70 + 68) = 53$

Q2. B = £11.97

$1.90 \times 7 = 13.30$

10% of 13.30 = 1.33

$13.30 - 1.33 = 11.97$

Q3. D = £0.12

$20 \times 5 = 100$

$12 \div 100 = 0.12$

Q4. E = £6.40

One box of pencils is £4.56 ÷ 3 = £1.52

$2 \times 1.52 = 3.04$

$3 \times 1.12 = 3.36$

$3.04 + 3.36 = 6.4$

Q5. D = 7:55 am

16 + 12 + 47 = 75 minutes/1 hour 15 minutes

6:40 am + 75 minutes = 7:55 am

Q6. A = 16.07 lbs

$22 - 1.7 - 1.5 - 0.5 - 1.98 - 0.25 = 16.07$

Q7. B = 135

0.18 (grams of fat per 1 gram of chocolate) × 750 = 135

Q8. E = 34

$85 \div 5 = 17$

$17 \times 2 = 34$

Q9. A = 2 mph

$1 \div 0.5 = 2$

Q10. C = £41.43

$100 - 14.45 - 11.35 - 32.77 = 41.43$

Q11. A = £38.13

$195 - 11.97 - 109.95 - 12.95 - 22 = 38.13$

Q12. E = £139.92

$12.95 + 85.99 + 17.99 + 22.99 = 139.92$

Q13. B = £875

$17,500 \div 100 = 175$

$175 \times 5 = 875$

Q14. B = 1,725 m

$69 \times 25 = 1,725$

Q15. C = 2:53 pm

$0.4 \times 72 = 288$ seconds

$288 \div 60 = 48$ minutes

2:05 pm + 48 minutes = 2:53 pm

Q16. B = 39

$18 \times 52 = 936$

$936 \div 24 = 39$

Q17. C = 42,900

$55,000 \div 100 = 550$

$550 \times 78 = 42,900$

Q18. A = 340

136 = 40%

$136 \div 40 = 3.4$

$3.4 \times 100 = 340$

Q19. A = 160

48 = 30%

$48 \div 30 = 1.6$

$1.6 \times 100 = 160$

Q20. D = £469.68

770 – 200 = 570

570 ÷ 5 = 114

114 × £4.12 = 469.68

Q21. B = 21.5 km

3 × 4 km/h = 12 km

1 × 3.5 km/h = 3.5 km

2 × 3 km/h = 6 km

12 + 3.5 + 6 = 21.5

Q22. B = 4 mph

3 ÷ 0.75 = 4

Q23. C = £2.61

2 hours 25 minutes = 145 minutes

145 ÷ 5 = 29

29 × £0.09 = £2.61

Q24. B = 22

18 × 6 = 108

240 – 108 = 132

132 ÷ 6 = 22

Q25. A = £2,637.90

97.70 × 12 = 1,172.4

1,172.4 × 3 = 3,517.2

3,517.2 ÷ 100 = 35.172

35.172 × 25 = 879.3

3,517.2 – 879.3 = 2,637.90

Q26. E = 210

8 – 2 = 6

6 × 5 = 30

30 × 7 = 210

Q27. B = 330

$3x$ – 115 = 875

$3x$ = 875 + 115

$3x$ = 990

990 ÷ 3 = 330

Q28. D = 11

$(5x – 15) ÷ 5 = 8$

$5x$ – 15 = 8 × 5

$5x$ – 15 = 40

$5x$ = 40 + 15

$5x$ = 55

55 ÷ 5 = 11

Q29. A = 18

$(9x – 122) ÷ 4 = 10$

$9x$ – 122 = 10 × 4

$9x$ – 122 = 40

$9x$ = 40 + 122

$9x$ = 162

162 ÷ 9 = 18

Q30. B = 7

$(7x – 5) ÷ 4 = 11$

$7x$ – 5 = 4 × 11

$7x$ – 5 = 44

$7x$ = 44 + 5

$7x$ = 49

49 ÷ 7 = 7

Basic 2

Question 1. What is 50% of 500, divided by 5?

[   ]

Question 2. What is 45% of 210, multiplied by 10?

[   ]

Question 3. What is 60% of 340, minus 27?

[   ]

Question 4. A flight leaves the airport at 22:00 hours. It is an 11 hour and 45-minute flight. There is a 2-hour time difference. What time will they arrive at their destination, assuming the time difference is 2 hours ahead?

[   ]

Question 5. A flight leaves the airport at 05:10 hours. It is a 17 hour and 15-minute flight. There is a 2-hour time difference. What time will they arrive at their destination, assuming the time difference is 2 hours behind?

[   ]

Question 6. A flight leaves the airport at 15:11 hours. It is a 22 hour and 10-minute flight. There is a 3-hour time difference. What time will they arrive at their destination, assuming the time difference is 3 hours ahead?

[   ]

Question 7. The clock below reads 3 am. How many degrees will the large (minute) hand have turned when the time reaches 3 pm? Circle your answer.

A	B	C	D	E
4,320°	360°	180°	90°	270°

Question 8. The clock below reads 3 pm. How many degrees will the large (minute) hand have turned when the time reaches 9 am? Circle your answer.

A	B	C	D	E
108°	7,560°	1,080°	6,480°	270°

Question 9. The clock below reads 3 pm. How many degrees will the small (hour) hand have turned when the time reaches 8 pm? Circle your answer.

A	B	C	D	E
210°	640°	1,270°	150°	270°

Question 10. The clock below reads 3 am. How many degrees will the small (hour) hand have turned when the time reaches 11 pm? Circle your answer.

A	B	C	D	E
600°	840°	210°	720°	690°

Question 11. The diagram below shows the plan of a building site. All angles are right angles. What is the area of the building site in m²? Circle your answer.

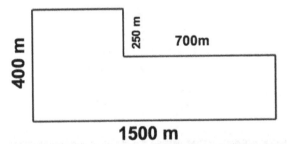

A	B	C	D	E
425,000 m²	225,000 m²	200,000 m²	2,850 m²	128,500 m²

Question 12. The diagram below shows the plan of a building site. All angles are right angles. What is the area of the building site in m²? Circle your answer.

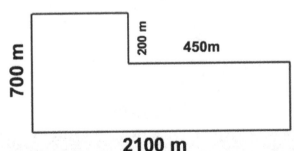

A	B	C	D	E
96,000 m²	1,380,000 m²	1,147,000 m²	420,000 m²	3,450 m²

Question 13. Which two numbers come next in the sequence? Circle your answer.

4, 2, 14, 12, 24, 22, ...

A	B	C	D	E
34, 32	32, 34	44, 52	52, 44	28, 26

Question 14. Which two numbers come next in the sequence? Circle your answer.

1, 11, 8, 18, 15, 25, ...

A	B	C	D	E
27, 45	27, 40	30, 35	22, 44	22, 32

Question 15. Which two numbers come next in the sequence? Circle your answer.

12, 10, 18, 16, 24, 22, ...

A	B	C	D	E
20, 28	30, 28	28, 32	32, 28	26, 28

Question 16. $40 \times 3 = 960 \div ?$

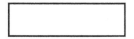

Question 17. $? \times 30 = 1{,}200 \div 8$

Question 18. $11 \times 22 = ? \div 121$

Question 19. $1{,}230 \div ? = 141 - 100$

Question 20. 1,266 – ? = 801 – 452

```
┌─────────────┐
│             │
│             │
└─────────────┘
```

Question 21. Mohammed is hiking in the Lake District. Using a compass, he discovers that he is facing North. If he turns 6 right angles anti-clockwise, what way will he be facing?

```
┌─────────────┐
│             │
│             │
└─────────────┘
```

Question 22. A family of 5 split the cost of all the household bills equally. The water bill was £120.40, the gas bill was £95.48, and the electric bill was £47.12. The rent for the month was £570. How much does each member of the family put towards covering all the bill costs?

```
┌─────────────┐
│             │
│             │
└─────────────┘
```

Question 23. Bill, Jonathan and Nadeem are out on the town having a few drinks to celebrate Bill's birthday. Bill buys 6 drinks at £3.95 each; Jonathan buys 8 drinks at £2.90 each and Nadeem buys 6 drinks at £3.40 each plus 3 packets of crisps at £0.90 each. Who spends the least amount?

```
┌─────────────┐
│             │
│             │
└─────────────┘
```

Question 24. Jessica, Rhonda, Shirley and Sebastian are out on the town having a few drinks to celebrate Christmas. Jessica buys 10 drinks at £3.95 each; Rhonda buys 10 drinks at £3.45 each plus 6 packets of nuts at £0.85 each; Sebastian buys 4 drinks at £3.40 each plus he paid the £26 taxi fare, and Shirley buys 12 drinks at £2.85 each plus 8 packets of crisps at £0.65 each. Who spends the least amount?

```
┌─────────────┐
│             │
│             │
└─────────────┘
```

Question 25. Richard is travelling from Kent to the Lake District. It is a 330-mile journey. If Richard sets off at 4:27 pm and averages 60 miles per hour for the entire journey, what time will he arrive at his destination?

```
┌─────────────┐
│             │
│             │
└─────────────┘
```

Question 26. A train travels 128 miles in 4 hours. What is the train's speed?

SCHOOL EXAM RESULT (Based on 200 pupils)				
Marks out of 80				
SUBJECT	0-19	20-39	40-59	60-80
Mathematics	37	41	57	65
English	34	41	43	82
Science	20	42	68	70
Geography	30	35	66	69

Question 27. Across all four subjects, how many results were less than 60 marks?

Question 28. In Mathematics, what percentage of pupils achieved marks of 60 or above?

Question 29. What is the percentage of pupils who achieved marks of 40 or above in their English exam?

Question 30. What was the average number of results with marks of 40 or above across all four subjects?

Answers to Basic 2

Q1. 50

$500 \div 100 = 5$

$5 \times 50 = 250$

$250 \div 5 = 50$

Q2. 945

$210 \div 100 = 2.1$

$2.1 \times 45 = 94.5$

$94.5 \times 100 = 945$

Q3. 177

$340 \div 100 = 3.4$

$3.4 \times 60 = 204$

$204 - 27 = 177$

Q4. 11:45 hours or 11:45 am

22:00 + 2 hours = 00:00

00:00 + 11 hours = 11:00

11:00 + 45 minutes = 11:45

Q5. 20:25 hours or 8:25 pm

05:10 + 17 hours 15 minutes = 22:25

22:25 − 2 hours = 20:25

Q6. 16:21 hours or 4:21 pm

15:11 + 3 hours = 18:11

18:11 + 10 minutes = 18:21

18:21 + 22 hours = 16:21

Q7. A = 4,320°

$360 \times 12 = 4,320$

Q8. D = 6,480°

$360 \times 18 = 6,480$

Q9. D = 150°

$360 \div 12 = 30$

$30 \times 5 = 150$

Q10. A = 600°

$360 \div 12 = 30$

$30 \times 20 = 600$

Q11. A = 425,000 m²

$400 \times 800 = 320,000$

$150 \times 700 = 105,000$

$320,000 + 105,000 = 425,000$

Q12. B = 1,380,000 m²

$1,650 \times 700 = 1,155,000$

$500 \times 450 = 225,000$

$1,155,000 + 225,000 = 1,380,000$

Q13. A = 34, 32

The sequence follows the format: −2, +12, −2, +12, −2, +12 etc.

Q14. E = 22, 32

The sequence follows the format: +10, −3, +10, −3, +10, −3 etc.

Q15. B = 30, 28

The sequence follows the format: −2, +8, −2, +8, −2, +8 etc.

Q16. 8

$40 \times 3 = 120$

$960 \div 120 = 8$

Q17. 5

$1,200 \div 8 = 150$

$150 \div 30 = 5$

Q18. 29,282

11 × 22 = 242

242 × 121 = 29,282

Q19. 30

141 − 100 = 41

1,230 ÷ 41 = 30

Q20. 917

801 − 452 = 349

1,266 − 349 = 917

Q21. South

6 × 90 = 540 = 1 full turn, plus a 180 degree turn = South

Q22. £166.60

120.40 + 95.48 + 47.12 + 570 = 833

833 ÷ 5 = 166.6

Q23. Nadeem

Bill = 3.95 × 6 = 23.70

Jonathan = 2.90 × 8 = 23.20

Nadeem = 3.4 × 6 = 20.40 + (0.90 × 3 = 2.70) = 23.10

Q24. Shirley

Jessica = 10 × 3.95 = 39.5

Rhonda = 10 × 3.45 = 34.5 + (6 × 0.85) = 39.6

Sebastian = 4 × 3.40 = 13.60 + 26 = 39.6

Shirley = 12 × 2.85 = 34.2 + (8 × 0.65) = 39.4

Q25. 9:57 pm

330 ÷ 60 = 5.5

4:27 pm + 5 hours 30 minutes = 9:57 pm

Q26. 32 mph

128 ÷ 4 = 32 mph

Q27. 514

37 + 41 + 57 + 34 + 41 + 43 + 20 + 42 + 68 + 30 + 35 + 66 =514

Q28. 32.5%

(65 ÷ 200) × 100 = 32.5

Q29. 62.5%

(125 ÷ 200) × 100 = 62.5

Q30. 130

57 + 65 + 43 + 82 + 68 + 70 + 66 + 69 = 520

520 ÷ 4 = 130

Function Machines

Question 1. A function is represented by the following machine.

$$10 \longrightarrow \boxed{\times 10} \longrightarrow \boxed{?} \quad 90$$

What is the missing function in the second part of the machine sequence?

A	B	C	D	E
− 10	− 12	× 1	÷ 5	+ 10

Question 2. A function is represented by the following machine.

$$88 \longrightarrow \boxed{\div 11} \longrightarrow \boxed{?} \quad 96$$

What is the missing function in the second part of the machine sequence?

A	B	C	D	E
× 10	− 12	× 12	÷ 1.2	+ 8

Question 3. A function is represented by the following machine.

$$7 \longrightarrow \boxed{\times 10} \longrightarrow \boxed{?} \quad 35$$

What is the missing function in the second part of the machine sequence?

A	B	C	D	E
× 5	× 3.5	− 30	− 35	+ 35

Question 4. A function is represented by the following machine.

$$40 \longrightarrow \boxed{\times 1} \longrightarrow \boxed{?} \quad 40$$

What is the missing function in the second part of the machine sequence?

A	B	C	D	E
× 1	× 10	÷ 10	÷ 2	+ 40

Question 5. A function is represented by the following machine.

100 — ÷ 5 — ? 2,000

What is the missing function in the second part of the machine sequence?

A	B	C	D	E
× 10	× 100	÷ 10	÷ 100	× 20

Question 6. A function is represented by the following machine.

100 — ? — × 20 400

What is the missing function in the first part of the machine sequence?

A	B	C	D	E
× 2	÷ 2	÷ 5	− 60	× 20

Question 7. A function is represented by the following machine.

9 — ? — × 2 162

What is the missing function in the first part of the machine sequence?

A	B	C	D	E
× 9	× 8	× 12	× 4	× 2

Question 8. A function is represented by the following machine.

12 — ? — × 5 720

What is the missing function in the first part of the machine sequence?

A	B	C	D	E
− 9	÷ 3	÷ 4	× 12	− 2

Question 9. A function is represented by the following machine.

1,250 — [?] — [÷ 75] 5

What is the missing function in the first part of the machine sequence?

A	B	C	D	E
$\sqrt{x}$	− 70%	÷ 75	+ 2%	− 50

Question 10. A function is represented by the following machine.

14 — [− 3] — [?] 121

What is the missing function in the second part of the machine sequence?

A	B	C	D	E
× 2.5	+ 100	x^2	× 25%	÷ 2.5

Question 11. A function is represented by the following machine.

81 — [$\sqrt{}$] — [?] 1

What is the missing function in the second part of the machine sequence?

A	B	C	D	E
− 80	+ 0.5	− 50%	− 8	÷ 2

Question 12. A function is represented by the following machine.

? — [× 2.5] — [÷ 10] 22

If the output of the machine is 22, what is the input?

A	B	C	D	E
2.2	88	250	120	25

Question 13. A function is represented by the following machine.

? — × 7 ▸ — ÷ 8 ▸ 224

If the output of the machine is 224, what is the input?

A	B	C	D	E
528	256	49	68	452

Question 14. A function is represented by the following machine.

? — x 7 ▸ — x 11 ▸ 616

If the output of the machine is 616, what is the input?

A	B	C	D	E
12	6	56	4	8

Question 15. A function is represented by the following machine.

? — ÷ 10 ▸ — x^2 ▸ 225

If the output of the machine is 225, what is the input?

A	B	C	D	E
2.25	225	150	350	2.5

Answers to Function Machines

Q1. A = − 10

10 × 10 = 100

100 − 90 = 10

Q2. C = × 12

88 ÷ 11 = 8

96 ÷ 8 = 12

8 × 12 = 96

Q3. D = − 35

7 × 10 = 70

70 − 35 = 35

Q4. A = × 1

40 × 1 = 40

Q5. B = × 100

100 ÷ 5 = 20

2,000 ÷ 20 = 100

20 × 100 = 2,000

Q6. C = ÷ 5

400 ÷ 20 = 20

20 × 5 = 100

Q7. A = × 9

162 ÷ 2 = 81

81 ÷ 9 = 9

Q8. D = × 12

720 ÷ 5 = 144

144 ÷ 12 = 12

Q9. B = − 70%

5 × 75 = 375

1250 ÷ 100 = 12.5

12.5 × 30 = 370

Q10. C = x^2

14 − 3 = 11

121 ÷ 11 = 11

Q11. D = − 8

$\sqrt{81}$ = 9

9 − 1 = 8

Q12. B = 88

22 × 10 = 220

220 ÷ 2.5 = 88

Q13. B = 256

224 × 8 = 1,792

1,792 ÷ 7 = 256

Q14. E = 8

616 ÷ 11 = 56

56 ÷ 7 = 8

Q15. C = 150

$\sqrt{225}$ = 15

15 × 10 = 150

Intermediate

Question 1. Write the following in the form $a\sqrt{b}$ where a and b are integers.

$$\sqrt{38} \times \sqrt{20}$$

Question 2. Work out the mode, median and mean of the following data set:

| 8 | 4 | -4 | -3 | 1 | 4 | 2 | 13 | 9 | 13 | -2 | 4 | 3 |

a) Mode [   ]   b) Median [   ]   c) Mean [   ]

Question 3. Make b the subject of the formula:

$$\sqrt{\frac{b + 9}{a}} = 12c$$

Question 4. Evaluate 8^{-4}. Leave your answer in fraction form.

Question 5. In any given week, the probabilities of Andy and Dave playing football are 0.5 and 0.3 respectively. Work out the probability that, in any given week, either Andy plays football, Dave plays football, or both play football.

Question 6. A straight line has a gradient of 4 and a y intercept of 6. Work out the equation of the line.

Question 7. Solve the following linear inequality:

$$2 - 6x \leq -8x - 4$$

Question 8. Fully simplify the following expression:

$$\frac{32a^3b^8}{8ab^4}$$

Question 9. Express the following expression as a single fraction and write this in its simplest form.

$$\frac{2(4y + 2)}{8y^2 - 4} - \frac{2}{4y + 1}$$

Question 10. Below is a right-angled triangle. Work out the length of side *AB*. Write your answer to the nearest whole number. You must show ALL of your working out.

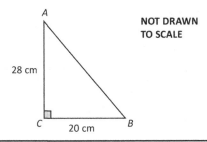

NOT DRAWN TO SCALE

Question 11. Find the coordinates of Point Z on the unit circle. Give your answer to 2 decimal places.

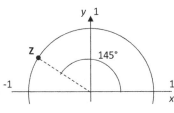

Question 12. Solve the simultaneous equation:

$$y = x^2 + 3 \text{ and } y - 2x = 18$$

Question 13. A square field, S, has an area greater than 2,916 m². Its length is decreased by 14 metres and its width is increased by 14 to give a rectangular field, R.

Which one of the following is true?

A. Area S < Area R and Perimeter S > Perimeter R

B. Area S > Area R and Perimeter S > Perimeter R

C. Area S = Area R and Perimeter S = Perimeter R

D. Area S < Area R and Perimeter S = Perimeter R

E. Area S > Area R and Perimeter S = Perimeter R

Question 14. A field is shown on a map. The field measures 6 cm by 8 cm on the map and the scale of the map is 1 : 6,000. Given that 10,000 m² is equivalent to 1 hectare, what is the area of the field in real life in hectares?

 A. 16 hectares **B.** 17.28 hectares **C.** 19 hectares **D.** 20.55 hectares **E.** 21 hectares

Question 15. The number of people with Malaria in Country A is 80% of the number of people with Malaria in Country B. The number of people with Malaria in Country C is 25% of that in Country A.

If the number of people with Malaria in Country C is 2350, what is the number of people with Malaria in Country B?

 A. 10,500   **B.** 13,750   **C.** 11,750   **D.** 11,500   **E.** 14,550

Question 16. The table shows the total tax paid in $ on annual taxable income. For example, a person with an annual taxable income of $60,000 will pay $4,990 plus 25% of ($60,000 - $36,250).

Annual Taxable Income Bracket ($)	Tax Rate	Total Tax paid at the top of this bracket ($)
0-8,950	10%	895
8,950-36,250	15%	4,990
36,250-87,850	25%	17,890
87,850-183,250	28%	44,602
183,250-400,000	33%	116,129.50
Over 400,000	39.6%	

Sam has an annual taxable income of $18,500. The income tax, to the nearest $, he has to pay is:

A. $2,328   B. $2,456   C. $2,139   D. $1,985   E. $3,457

Question 17. The following graph shows the velocity of two cars at different times.

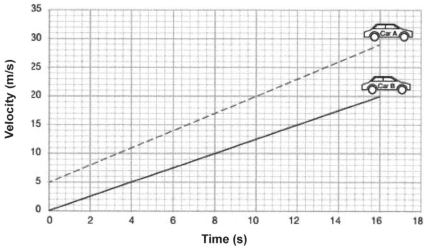

How much greater is the acceleration of Car A than the acceleration of Car B?

Acceleration (m/s²) = Change in velocity (m/s) / Change in time (s)

A. 1.83 m/s²   B. 0.25 m/s²   C. 0.53 m/s²   D. 1.73 m/s²   E. 0.63 m/s²

Question 18. The maximum amounts any family can claim for "Basic Working Tax Credits", "Severe Disability Tax Credits" and "Child Tax Credits" are £1,940, £1,255 and £545 respectively.

Suppose a family is eligible to claim 70% of the maximum tax credits in each category. What is the total amount of tax credits the family can claim?

A. £2,618   B. £3,119   C. £2,186   D. £1,628   E. £1,268

Question 19. Kent Police have put out a notice for staff to enrol onto training courses. Below are quotes from 3 suppliers.

Academic training course	College 1 Total cost over 4 years (£)	College 2 Total cost over 2 years (£)	College 3 Total cost over 6 years (£)
PR and Advertising	14,500	8,350	34,500
Finances	18,250	8,750	42,750
Social Media	24,050	13,000	72,000

What percentage of the total quote provided by College 2 accounts for Social Media training?

A. 40.1%   B. 45.6%   C. 43.2%   D. 44.5%

Question 20. Place the numbers from 1 to 9 in each square. Each number should only be used once. The number in the circle should equal the sum of the four surrounding squares. Pay attention to the colour of the squares. Each colour needs to represent the total as shown in the coloured circles next to the grid.

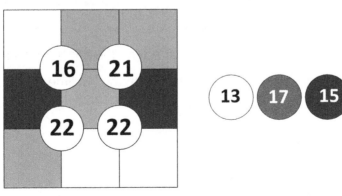

Answers to Intermediate

Q1. $2\sqrt{190}$

$\sqrt{38} \times \sqrt{20} = \sqrt{(38 \times 20)} = \sqrt{760}$

However when simplifying surds you are often asked to go a step further by looking for square factors. In this example 760 has a factor of 4 because $4 \times 190 = 760$. We can now write that $\sqrt{760} = \sqrt{(4 \times 190)} = \sqrt{4} \times \sqrt{190}$.

Now because $\sqrt{4}=2$, so we can rewrite this again: $\sqrt{4} \times \sqrt{190} = 2\sqrt{190}$.

Q2. a) 4

The number that occurs the most number of times is 4.

b) 4

If you put all the numbers in ascending order, and find the 'middle' number, you will reach the answer of 4.

c) 4

To work out the mean, you need to add up all of the numbers, and then divide it by how many numbers there are. $52 \div 13 = 4$

Q3. $b = 144ac^2 - 9$

Square both sides to get rid of the square root $= (b + 9) \div a = (12c)^2$

Multiply by a to get rid of the fraction $= b + 9 = 144ac^2$

Collect all the terms without b on the right-hand side by subtracting 9:

$b = 144ac^2 - 9$

Q4. $\dfrac{1}{4,096}$

$8^{-4} = \dfrac{1}{8^4} = \dfrac{1}{4,096}$

Q5. 0.65

P("Andy plays OR Dave plays") $= 0.5 + 0.3 - 0.15 = 0.65$.

So, P(A or D) $= 0.5 + 0.3 - 0.15 = 0.65$

Q6. $y = 4x + 6$

The gradient is 4, and the y-intercept is 6.

So, $y = 4x + 6$

Q7. $x \leq -3$

$2 - 6x \leq -8x - 4$ so $2x \leq -6$ so $x \leq -3$

Q8. $4a^2b^4$

First, divide the numbers: $32 \div 8 = 4 = \dfrac{4a^3b^8}{ab^4}$

Next, cancel the common factor a: $\dfrac{4a^2b^8}{b^4}$

Apply exponent rule: $x^a \div x^b = x^{a-b}$

$b^8 \div b^4 = b^8 - 4 = b^4$

So the answer is $4a^2b^4$

Q9. $\dfrac{4y^2 + 6y + 3}{8y^3 + 2y^2 - 4y - 1}$

$\dfrac{2(4y^2 + 2)}{8y^2 - 4} - \dfrac{2}{4y + 1}$

$= \dfrac{16y^2 + 24y + 12}{32y^3 + 8y^2 - 16y - 4}$

$= \dfrac{4y^2 + 6y + 3}{8y^3 + 2y^2 - 4y - 1}$

Q10. 34 cm

ACB = right angle

AC = 28 cm

BC = 20 cm

$AB^2 = 28^2 + 20^2$

$= 784 + 400 = 1{,}184$

$= \sqrt{1{,}184} = 34.4093\ldots$

To the nearest whole number = 34 cm.

Q11. (−0.82, 0.57)

Point Z is on the unit circle.

The x coordinate is cos 145° = −0.81915...

The y coordinate is sin 145° = 0.57357...

So, the coordinates of Point Z to 2 d.p. are (−0.82, 0.57)

Q12. x = −3 and y = 12 OR x = 5 and y = 28

Q13. E

The area of S will be larger than the area of R. The perimeter of S and R will remain the same.

Q14. B

Q15. C

Q16. A

Q17. B

Q18. A

Q19. C = 43.2%

13,000 + 8,750 + 8,350 = 30,100

13,000 ÷ 30,100 × 100 = 43.18%

Rounded to 43.2%

Q20.

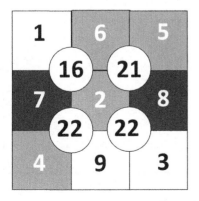

Advanced

Question 1. C is a curve. This curve has the equation $4y^3 + 20y + 4 = x$

Find $\dfrac{dy}{dx}$ in terms of y.

Question 2. Given that $\sin\theta = \dfrac{\sqrt{6}}{4}$, find the exact value of $\sin 6\theta$.

Question 3. Work out how many integers, n, where $0 \le n < 1{,}000$ are NOT divisible by 2 or 5.

Question 4. Solve the simultaneous equations:

$$3x - 2y = 9 \text{ and } x + 4y = 10$$

Question 5. A dance battle is arranged for $2n$ dancers. The tournament sees only the winners in any given round proceed to the next stage. Opponents in each round except the final are drawn at random, and in any match either player has a probability 0.5 of winning. Two dancers are chosen at random before the first round.

Work out the probability in terms of n that they will compete against each other in the first round.

Question 6. Show that, in the diagram below, $\cos \alpha = \dfrac{63}{65}$

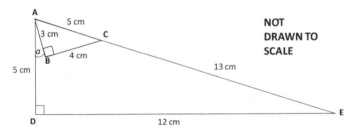

NOT
DRAWN TO
SCALE

Question 7. In triangle ABC, $\overrightarrow{AB} = 4i - 3j$ and $\overrightarrow{AC} = i - 3j$

Work out the value of <BAC in degrees to 1 d.p.

Question 8. Write $6x^2 - 4x = -4$ in the form $p(x + q)^2 + r = 0$

Question 9. Find the length AC in the triangle below. Write your answer to 1 decimal place.

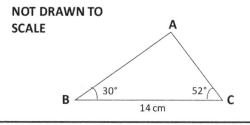

NOT DRAWN TO SCALE

30° 52°

B   14 cm   C

A

Question 10. Solve the simultaneous equations:

$$y = 14 - x \text{ and } x - y = 8$$

Question 11. A straight line $y = 4x - 8$ meets the x-axis at point A. Work out the equation of the line with gradient ⅓ that passes through point A.

Write your answer in the form $ax + by + c = 0$, where a, b and c are integers.

Question 12. A cuboid box is made from 63 m² of cardboard. The box has a horizontal base and no top. The height of the box is x metres. The two opposite vertical faces are squares.

Show that the volume of the box is given by $V = 21x - \dfrac{2}{3} x^3$

Question 13. Find the coordinates of the stationary points on the curve with the following equation:

$$y = \frac{2}{3} x^3 - 12x^2 + 20x + 2$$

Question 14. If $4x - y = 16$, what is the value of $\dfrac{16^x}{2^y}$?

Question 15. Evaluate the sum $\displaystyle\sum_{10}^{20} (6b - 4)$

Question 16. Here is some information about the costs of purchasing land.

Prime farmland is £6,500 per acre. Building land is £1.2 million per hectare. The table shows the costs, in thousands of pounds per hectare, of cleaning sites. These are paid in addition to cost of purchasing the land.

End Use	Previous Use	Factories	Sewage works	Scrapyards	Steel works Chemical works
Open space	80	200	400	395
Residential	150	350	500	475
Employment	80	200	175	450
Mixed use	90	258	465	395

1 hectare = 10,000 m² = 2.47 acres.

Building developers buy an old sewage works with an area of 4 acres. They intend to clean the site for residential use. They know they can use an area 1/10th of an acre for a house.

Work out the total cost, to the nearest £, of buying and cleaning the land per house.

Question 17. Find positive integers a and b such that $3a + 7b = 29$.

Question 18. Below is an image of an enclosure. If the length of the diagonal *BD* is 80 metres, work out the angle between the fences *AB* and *BC*.

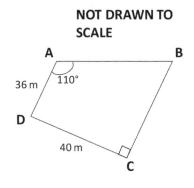

NOT DRAWN TO SCALE

Question 19. Here is some information about the costs of purchasing land. Prime farmland is £7,500 per acre. Building land is £1.1 million per hectare. The table shows the costs, in thousands of pounds per hectare, of cleaning sites. These are paid in addition to the cost of purchasing the land.

End Use	Previous Use	Factories	Sewage works	Scrapyards	Steel works Chemical works
Open space		80	200	400	395
Residential		150	350	500	475
Employment		80	200	175	450
Mixed use		90	258	465	395

1 hectare = 10,000 m² = 2.47 acres

How many whole hectares of prime farmland could be bought for the total cost of buying a one hectare derelict sewage works and cleaning it for residential use?

Question 20. The mean of a set of 10 numbers is 50. The mean of another set of 12 numbers is 42.

Work out the combined mean of both sets of numbers. Write your answer to 2 d.p.

Answers to Advanced

Q1. $\dfrac{dy}{dx} = \dfrac{1}{12y^2 + 20}$

$x = 4y^3 + 20y + 4$

$\dfrac{dy}{dx} = (4 \times 3)y^{3-1} + 20y^{1-1} + 0$

$\dfrac{dy}{dx} = 12y^2 + 20$

$\dfrac{dy}{dx} = \dfrac{1}{12y^2 + 20}$

Q2. $-\dfrac{3}{16}\sqrt{15}$

$\sin 6\theta = \sin 2(3\theta)$

Using the double angle formula $\sin 2x = 2 \sin x \cos x$ to expand $\sin 2(3\theta)$

$\sin 6\theta = 2 \sin 3\theta \cos 3\theta$

Using the triple angle formula $\sin 3x = 3 \sin x - 4 \sin^3 x$ and $\cos 3x = 4 \cos^3 x - 3 \cos x$ to expand $\sin 3\theta$ and $\cos 3\theta$

$\sin 6\theta = 2(3 \sin\theta - 4 \sin^3 \theta)(4 \cos^3 \theta - 3 \cos \theta)$

Given that $\sin \theta = \dfrac{\sqrt 6}{4}$, then $\cos \theta = \dfrac{\sqrt{10}}{4}$

$\sin 6\theta = 2 \left(3\left(\dfrac{\sqrt 6}{4}\right) - 4 \left(\dfrac{\sqrt 6}{4}\right)^3\right) \left(4\left(\dfrac{\sqrt{10}}{4}\right)^3 - 3 \left(\dfrac{\sqrt{10}}{4}\right)\right) = -\dfrac{3}{16}\sqrt{15}$

Q3. 400

Integers ending in 1, 3, 7 or 9 will not be divisible by 2 or 5. This is equivalent to $\frac{4}{10}$.

The total number of integers is $\frac{4}{10}$ of 1,000 = 400.

Q4. $x = 4$ and $y = 1.5$

Begin by multiplying the equation $x + 4y = 10$ by 3 so that we have the same coefficient of x with the first equation

Equation 1: $3x - 2y = 9$

Equation 2: $3x + 12y = 30$ (after multiplying each term by 3)

Subtract Equation 1 from Equation 2, we have:

$12y - (-2y) = 30 - 9$

$14y = 21$

$y = {}^{21}\!/_{14} = 1.5$

Substitute the value $y = 1.5$ back into the first equation

$3x - (2 \times 1.5) = 9$

$3x - 3 = 9$

$3x = 12$

$x = 4$

Q5. $\dfrac{1}{2^{2n} - 2^{n}}$

The probability of picking the first dancer, D1, is $\dfrac{1}{2^{n}}$

The probability of picking the second dancer, D2, is $\dfrac{1}{2^{n} - 1}$

The probability of these two dancers competing against each other is:

$$\dfrac{1}{2^{n}} \times \dfrac{1}{2^{n} - 1} = \dfrac{1}{2^{2n} - 2^{n}}$$

Q6. $\dfrac{63}{65}$

Using the two right-angled triangles you can determine the following trigonometric ratios:

$$\sin\angle DAE = \frac{12}{13}, \qquad \cos\angle DAE = \frac{5}{13}$$

$$\sin\angle BAC = \frac{4}{5}, \qquad \cos\angle BAC = \frac{3}{5}$$

Now since $a = \angle DAE - \angle BAC$, we can use the angle subtraction formula for cosine to find $\cos a$:

$$\cos a = \cos(\angle DAE - \angle BAC)$$

$$= \cos\angle DAE \times \cos\angle BAC + \sin\angle DAE \times \sin\angle BAC$$

$$= \frac{5}{13} \times \frac{3}{5} + \frac{12}{13} \times \frac{4}{5}$$

$$= \frac{15}{65} + \frac{48}{65}$$

$$= \frac{63}{65}$$

Q7. 34.7°

First find the dot product $\vec{AB} \cdot \vec{AC}$:

$\vec{AB} \cdot \vec{AC} = (4 \times 1) + (-3x\ -3) = 4 + 9 = 13$

$\vec{AB} = \sqrt{4^2 + (-3)^2} = \sqrt{25} = 5$ and $\vec{AC} = \sqrt{1^2 + (-3)^2} = \sqrt{10}$. Use the identity $\vec{AB}$

$\vec{AC} = \vec{AB}\ \vec{AC} \cos\theta$, where θ is the angle between the vectors:

$5\sqrt{10} \cos\theta = 13$

$\theta = \cos^{-1} \dfrac{13}{5\sqrt{10}} \approx 34.7°$

Q8. $6(x - \frac{1}{3})^2 + \frac{10}{3} = 0$

$6x^2 - 4x + 4 = 0$

$6(x^2 - \frac{2}{3}x) + 4 = 0$

$(x - \frac{1}{3})^2 = x^2 - \frac{2}{3}x + \frac{1}{9}$, can be rewritten $x^2 - \frac{2}{3}x$ as $(x - \frac{1}{3})^2 - \frac{1}{9}$

$6(x - \frac{1}{3})^2 - \frac{1}{9} + 4 = 0$

$6(x - \frac{1}{3})^2 - \frac{10}{3} = 0$

Q9. 7.1 cm

Angle BAC = 180 − (30 + 52) = 98°

$\frac{AC}{\sin 30} = \frac{14}{\sin 98}$

$AC = \frac{14}{\sin 98} \times \sin 30$

AC = 7.1 (rounded to 1 d.p.)

Q10. x = 11 and y = 3

$x - (14 - x) = 8$

$x - 14 + x = 8$

$2x - 14 = 8$

$2x = 8 + 14$

$2x = 22$

$x = 11$

You can substitute x = 11 into the equations to confirm that y = 3

Q11. $-x + 3y + 2 = 0$ or $x - 3y - 2 = 0$

$0 = 4x - 8$ So $x = 2$. A is the point (2, 0).

$3y = x - 2$

$-x + 3y + 2 = 0$

Q12. $V = 21x - \dfrac{2}{3} x^3$

Area $= 2x^2 + 3xy$

$63 = 2x^2 + 3xy$

$y = \dfrac{63 - 2x^2}{3x}$

$V = x^2 (\dfrac{63 - 2x^2}{3x})$

$V = \dfrac{x}{3} (63 - 2x^2)$

$V = 21x - \dfrac{2}{3} x^3$

Q13. $(6 + \sqrt{26}, -342.8)$ and $(6 - \sqrt{26}, 10.8)$

$y = \dfrac{2}{3} x^3 - 12x^2 + 20x + 2$

$\dfrac{dy}{dx} = (\dfrac{2}{3} \times 3)x^{3-1} - (12 \times 2)^{2-1} + (20 \times 1)x^{1-1} + 0$

$\dfrac{dy}{dx} = 2x^2 - 24 x^1 + 20$

$\dfrac{dy}{dx} = 0 \Rightarrow 2x^2 - 24x + 20 = 0$

$\Rightarrow x^2 - 12x + 10 = 0$

$\Rightarrow x = \dfrac{12 \pm \sqrt{(-12)^2 - 4 \times 10}}{2}$

$\Rightarrow x = 6 \pm \sqrt{26}$

$y_1 = \dfrac{2}{3} (6 + \sqrt{26})^3 - 12(6 + \sqrt{26})^2 + 20(6 + \sqrt{26}) + 2 = -342.8$

$y_2 = \dfrac{2}{3} (6 - \sqrt{26})^3 - 12(6 - \sqrt{26})^2 + 20(6 - \sqrt{26}) + 2 = -10.8$

Q14. 2^{16}

$$\frac{16^x}{2^y} = \frac{(2^4)^x}{2^y} = \frac{2^{4x}}{2^y} = 2^{(4x-y)} = \frac{16^x}{2^y} = 2^{16}$$

Q15. 946

$$\sum_{b=10}^{20} (6b-4) = (6\sum_{r=1}^{20} r - \sum_{r=1}^{20} 4) - 6\sum_{r=1}^{9} r - \sum_{r=1}^{9} 4)$$

$$(\frac{6}{2} \times 20(21) - 4 \times 20) - (\frac{6}{2} \times 9(10) - 4 \times 9)$$

$$= (1{,}290 - 80) - (270 - 36)$$

$$= 1{,}180 - 234 = 946$$

Q16. £62,753

Number of houses = 4 acres ÷ $\frac{1}{10}$ = 40 houses.

4 acres = $\frac{4}{2.47}$ hectare.

Cost of buying = 1,200,000 × $\frac{4}{2.47}$ = £1,943,319.84

Cost of cleaning = 350,000 × $\frac{4}{2.47}$ = 566,801.62

Total cost = 1,943,319.84 + 566,801.62 = £2,510,121.46

Total cost per house = 2,510,121.46 ÷ 40 = £62,753.04

To the nearest pound = £62,753

Q17. $a = 5$, $b = 2$

To solve this, start by considering the possible values of b. We know that b is positive, and $b < 5$, since 5 × 7 = 35, which is greater than 29.

If $b = 1$, then $7b = 7$, so $3a + 7 = 29$ meaning $3a = 22$. This cannot have an integer solution for a, as 22 is not a multiple of 3.

If $b = 2$, then $7b = 7 \times 2 = 14$, so $3a + 14 = 29$ meaning $3a = 15$. This has solution $a = 5$. So a possible pair of positive integers a, and b, such that $3a + 7b = 29$ is $a = 5$, $b = 2$.

There are no other positive integer solutions for a and b to this equation, since if $b = 3$, $3a = 8$, and if $b = 4$, $3a = 1$. Neither of these possibilities has an integer solution for a.

Q18. 55.0°

$$\sin\angle DBC = \frac{40}{80}$$

$$\angle DBC = \sin^{-1} 0.5$$

$$= 30$$

$$\frac{\sin\angle ABD}{36} = \frac{\sin 110°}{80}$$

$$\sin\angle ABD = \frac{36\sin 110°}{80}$$

$$\angle ABD = \sin^{-1}\left(\frac{36\sin 110°}{80}\right) = 25.01$$

Then $\angle ABC = \angle DBC + \angle ABD = 30° + 25.01° = 55.0°$ to 1 d.p.

Q19. 78

Total cost of buying and cleaning is 1,100,000 + 350,000 = 1,450,000 for one hectare.

If total cost is £1,450,000 for one hectare, then the total cost is also £1,450,000 for 2.47 acres (since 1 hectare = 2.47 acres). Total cost for one acre is 1,450,000 ÷ 2.47 = £587,044.53

Number of farmland could be bought in acres is £587,044.53 ÷ £7,500 = 78.27

The number of whole hectares would be 78.

Q20. 45.64

$$\frac{10 \times 50 + 12 \times 42}{10 + 12} = \frac{1,004}{22} = 45,636$$

To 2 d.p. = 45.64

Verbal Reasoning

Verbal Reasoning tests are designed to challenge your knowledge of words, the relationship between different words, and your general English language competency. Below, we have listed some of the most common/typical tests that you will encounter during a Verbal Reasoning Assessment, and provided you with examples of how each type of question can be answered.

Antonyms and Synonyms

Antonym and Synonym questions are commonly used in Verbal Reasoning assessments. They challenge your understanding of different words and what they mean. Before we look at the questions, let's take a look at what both of these terms actually mean:

Antonym. An antonym can be defined as a word that is opposite in meaning to another. So, if you are given the word 'good', then the antonym of this would be 'bad'. If you were given the word 'wet', then the antonym of this would be 'dry'.

Synonym. Synonyms work in a similar way. A synonym is a word which means 'nearly or exactly the same' as another word. So, if you are given the word 'evil' then one synonym of this would be 'reprehensible'. Another might be 'machiavellian'. If you were given the word 'hungry' then a synonym of this might be 'famished'. You can see here that there is a difference between these two terms. 'Famished' is a word which means extreme hunger, whereas if you are just 'hungry' then you are not necessarily 'famished', but the words are similar, and therefore act as synonyms.

Now, let's look at a few example questions, to illustrate the type of thing that would be expected of you when answering these exercises:

Which of the following is a synonym of **Strange**:

A - Barren | B - Hostile | C - Perpendicular | D - Alien | E - Suave

Answer = D - Alien.

The term 'strange' refers to something unusual or unexpected, different from the norm. Likewise, the term 'alien' can be used to describe something that is unfamiliar or disturbing. Therefore, these two words are synonyms.

Now, let's look at another sample question:

Which of the following is an antonym of **Best:**

A - Worst | B - Last | C - Loser | D - Failure | E - Closest

Answer = A - Worst

In this case, the direct antonym to 'Best' is 'Worst', which is answer option A. Notice how sometimes the question will try to trip you up, using words which could be closely related/or almost opposite, but aren't quite as good as other options.

True, False, Or Impossible To Say

True, False, Or Impossible To Say questions are commonly seen during Verbal Reasoning tests, and test your reading comprehension skills, plus your attention to detail.

In these questions, you'll generally be given a passage, and will then need to answer a series of statements following the passage with True, False or Impossible To Say.

Here's a quick refresher on what is meant by True, False, and Impossible To Say in the context of the Verbal Reasoning test.

TRUE - If a statement is 'true', then it can be verified by the text. This means that the text must explicitly or implicitly mention something which proves the statement to be correct. In other words, you cannot make any assumptions about the text. There must either be direct evidence for the statement, or a strong inference to support the statement.

FALSE - If a statement is 'false', there must be evidence in the text which contradicts the statement. For example, if the question statement says 'all swans are white', but the text says 'there is such a thing as a black swan', then the statement is false because it is directly contradicted by the text.

IMPOSSIBLE TO SAY - If there is not enough evidence to verify that the statement is true or false, then the correct answer is 'impossible to say'. Simply put, this means that you cannot say the statement is true or false based on the information provided in the passage.

To give you an idea of what these types of test look like, let's have a look at an example question:

Sample Passage

People pay National Insurance contributions in order to build up their entitlement to a state pension and other social security benefits. The amount that you pay is directly linked to the amount you earn. If you earn over a certain amount, your employer deducts Class 1 National Insurance contributions from your wages through the PAYE system. You pay a lower rate of National Insurance contributions if you're a member of your employer's 'contracted-out' pension scheme, or you're a married woman – or widow – who holds a valid 'election certificate'. Your employer also pays employer National Insurance contributions based on your earnings and on any benefits you get with your job, for example a company car. HMRC keeps track of your contributions through your National Insurance number. This is like an account number and is unique to you.

Q1a. People pay National Insurance contributions in order to build up housing benefits.

TRUE | FALSE | IMPOSSIBLE TO SAY

Answer = Impossible To Say

Although the statement makes reference to social security benefits, it does not confirm that these include housing benefits. The correct answer is impossible to say based on the information provided.

Q1b. An employer pays employer National Insurance contributions if an employee has a company car.

TRUE | FALSE | IMPOSSIBLE TO SAY

Answer = True

The passage states that "Your employer also pays employer National Insurance contributions based on your earnings and on any benefits you get with your job, for example a company car". The statement is true.

Tenses

During Verbal Reasoning, it is very common to encounter tense related questions. These are questions which focus around your understanding of past, present and future tense, and the way tense related phrasing works in sentences. Before we go any further, let's take a look at the three different tenses used in writing:

Past Tense. In very simple terms, the past tense is used to refer to the past. It explains what has happened already, or what has already existed. The most common indicator that something is written in the past tense, is the word 'was'.

Here are some examples of the past tense:

'Yesterday morning, I walked to work.'

This is an easy one - we can see from the term 'yesterday' that the event referred to is in the past. It happened the day before today - yesterday - and therefore we know that the rest of the sentence will need to be written in the past tense too. With this in mind, the verb adds an (ed). 'Walk' becomes 'walked'.

Now let's look at another example:

'I was sent to prison, for a crime I did not commit.'

In this sentence, the phrase 'was' gives us an indication that the sentence is written in the past tense. Was is the past tense version of 'be', and refers to something that has already happened. 'He was sitting down', 'She was standing up.'

Present Tense. In very simple terms, the present tense is used to refer to something that is currently happening, existing, or taking place. The most common indicator that something is written in the present tense, is the use of the word 'is'.

Here are some examples of the present tense:

'It is extremely sunny right now, I'm too hot.'

In this sentence, you can see that the word 'is' lends itself to demonstrating that this is written in the present tense. The use of the phrase 'I'm' also indicates that this is happening in the present tense.

Here's another example of a sentence written in the present tense:

'I'm currently on my way to the supermarket.'

In this sentence, the use of the word 'currently' indicates that it is written in present tense. 'Currently' refers to the present, something that is currently happening.

Future Tense. In very simple terms, the future tense is used to refer to something that will happen in the future. It explains what will happen, at a future point in time. The most common indicator that something is written in the future tense, is the term 'will'.

Here are some examples of the future tense:

'Today, I will go to the shops, and buy bread.'

In this sentence, the use of the phrase 'will' indicates that said event is yet to happen, and therefore will happen in the future.

'Next year, I shall be swimming for Britain, at the Olympics.'

In this sentence, the phrase 'shall be' indicates that the activity will be happening in the future.

Obviously, this is a very simple breakdown of just the three main tenses. There are lots of rules when it comes to tenses, which can be confusing for newcomers to the language, and even to natural English speakers. For more advice on specific tenses, and variations on tenses, check out our grammar guides on www.How2Become. com.

Now, let's look at some sample tense related questions.

Sample Question 1

Identify which tense the below sentence is written in:

On Monday, I went to the shops. My brother came with me. He purchased eight bottles of whiskey.

Sample Question 2

Identify which of the answer options best fits in the below sentence:

Tomorrow morning, I _____ play football with my friends. We are going to beat the other team, and then ____ ice cream.

A - will, bought

B - won't, buy

C - did, purchased

D - will, buy

Answers

Q1. Answer = Past tense.

This sentence is written in the past tense, as demonstrated by the words 'went', 'came' and 'purchased'.

Q2. Answer = D.

This sentence is written in the future tense, as demonstrated by the words/phrases 'tomorrow', 'play', 'are going' and 'beat'. Therefore, the words which best fit in this sentence are 'will' (future tense) and 'buy' (future tense).

Word Grids

Question 1. Start at one of the corners and move clockwise around the square finishing in the centre to create a nine-letter word.

I		Y
T	K	
	D	R

Question 2. Start at one of the corners and move clockwise around the square finishing in the centre to create a nine-letter word.

A		Q
	D	
	T	I

Question 3. Start at one of the corners and move clockwise around the square finishing in the centre to create a nine-letter word.

B		L
U	M	
	U	G

Question 4. Start at one of the corners and move anti-clockwise around the square finishing in the centre to create a nine-letter word.

P		E
H	E	S
	S	

Question 5. Start at one of the corners and move anti-clockwise around the square finishing in the centre to create a nine-letter word.

	I	L
K	S	F
	U	

Question 6. Start at one of the corners and move anti-clockwise around the square finishing in the centre to create a nine-letter word.

	O	L
	E	Y
O	N	

Question 7. Start at one of the corners and move clockwise around the square finishing in the centre to create a nine-letter word.

	E	P
	D	E
L	A	

Question 8. Start at one of the corners and move anti-clockwise around the square finishing in the centre to create a nine-letter word.

I		O
	E	M
G	L	

Question 9. Start at one of the corners and move clockwise around the square finishing in the centre to create a nine-letter word.

O		C
	G	U
I	Y	

Question 10. Start at one of the corners and move anti-clockwise around the square finishing in the centre to create a nine-letter word.

U		E
	E	L
T	A	

> EQUITABLE

Question 11. Start at one of the corners and move clockwise around the square finishing in the centre to create a nine-letter word.

E		I
E		
U		S

> SQUEEZING

Question 12. Start at one of the corners and move anti-clockwise around the square finishing in the centre to create a nine-letter word.

B		N
A	H	E
	K	

> BACKBENCH

Question 13. Start at one of the corners and move clockwise around the square finishing in the centre to create a nine-letter word.

I		V
	E	U
A	C	

Question 14. Start at one of the corners and move anti-clockwise around the square finishing in the centre to create a nine-letter word.

Q	N	A
I	C	

Question 15. Start at one of the corners and move anti-clockwise around the square finishing in the centre to create a nine-letter word.

I		T
S		A
E	M	

Answers to Word Grids

Q1. Yardstick

Q2. Acquitted

Q3. Bubblegum

Q4. Emphasise

Q5. Cufflinks

Q6. Xylophone

Q7. Penalised

Q8. Glamorise

Q9. Occupying

Q10. Equitable

Q11. Squeezing

Q12. Backbench

Q13. Vulcanise

Q14. Quicksand

Q15. Empathise

Letter Combinations

Question 1. Which 3 of the 8 letter bits can be combined to create a word meaning eat or drink (something) greedily?

ZLI, GED, SCO, ING, FIN, GUZ, EAT, NG

```
┌─────────────────────────────────────┐
│                                      │
│                                      │
│                                      │
└─────────────────────────────────────┘
```

Question 2. Which 3 of the 8 letter bits can be combined to create a word referring to someone being childish or immature?

RET, JUV, RED, DED, IMM, AR, EN, ILE

```
┌─────────────────────────────────────┐
│                                      │
│                                      │
│                                      │
└─────────────────────────────────────┘
```

Question 3. Which 3 of the 8 letter bits can be combined to create a word that means 'showing impressive beauty'?

BEA, JES, SMA, UT, TIC, IF, UL, MA

```
┌─────────────────────────────────────┐
│                                      │
│                                      │
│                                      │
└─────────────────────────────────────┘
```

Question 4. Which 3 of the 8 letter bits can be combined to create a word that means 'to alter or move (something) slightly in order to achieve the desired fit'?

EDS, ADJ, CHA, ING, OVE, ERD, UST, URT

```
┌─────────────────────────────────────┐
│                                      │
│                                      │
│                                      │
└─────────────────────────────────────┘
```

Question 5. Which 3 of the 8 letter bits can be combined to create a word that means 'to cause (two or more things) to exchange places'?

OSE, ALT, ERI, TRA, ED, RED, UST, NSP

Question 6. Which 3 of the 8 letter bits can be combined to create a word that means 'to keep something afloat or to describe something rising to the top of a liquid or gas'?

BOU, FLO, BUO, TRA, YA, ATE, RES, NT

Question 7. Which 3 of the 8 letter bits can be combined to create a word that describes a formal religious or public occasion?

MEE, ONY, TIN, GED, CHE, WAT, REM, CE

Question 8. Which 3 of the 8 letter bits can be combined to create a word that describes having power and influence over others?

DO, ANT, FOR, CED, FED, MIN, FLE, CE

Question 9. Which 3 of the 8 letter bits can be combined to create a word that describes objects that are side by side and have the same distance continuously between them?

RAL, STR, AIG, ERT, HER, LIN, LEL, PA

Question 10. Which 3 of the 8 letter bits can be combined to create a word that describes what someone becomes when they decide they do not want to communicate with other people?

HDR, WIT, LST, PUL, LIS, TEN, DER, AWN

Question 11. Which 3 of the 8 letter bits can be combined to create a word meaning a person who is travelling or visiting a place for pleasure?

TUO, VIS, ST, ING, ITO, RSE, URI, TO

Question 12. Which 3 of the 8 letter bits can be combined to create a word to describe a shoe with a thin, high tapering heel?

LLE, STI, HEE, ING, LET, ELS, SHO, TO

Question 13. Which 4 of the 8 letter bits can be combined to create a word to describe a pneumatic or electro-mechanical tool that combines a hammer directly with a chisel?

MM, CHI, SEL, JAC, ER, MER, HAM, KHA

Question 14. Which 4 of the 8 letter bits can be combined to create a word to describe a firm white Italian cheese made from buffalo or cow's milk?

MO, REL, CHE, EES, REN, LA, BRE, ZZA

Question 15. Which 4 of the 8 letter bits can be combined to create a word to describe having or showing a dislike of or prejudice against people from other countries?

NOP, RAC, HOB, ISM, IA, XE, EXT, ZZA

Question 16. Which 4 of the 8 letter bits can be combined to create a word to describe accepting something reluctantly but without protest?

QUI, CE, EPT, ACC, AC, AR, ING, ES

Question 17. Which 4 of the 8 letter bits can be combined to create a word to describe a person who helps another commit a crime?

ICE, ACC, RED, DER, MON, NED, PL, OM

Question 18. Which 4 of the 8 letter bits can be combined to create a word to describe a huge, powerful, and overwhelming force?

GER, PLE, MEN, UT, NA, UTE, ARN, JUG

Question 19. Which 3 of the 8 letter bits can be combined to create a word to describe putting off or postponing (a resolution or sentence)?

POS, ADJ, POT, RN, MEN, DIN, NE, OU

Question 20. Which 4 of the 8 letter bits can be combined to create a word to describe the quality of being full of energy, excitement, and cheerfulness?

RA, MEN, NCE, MED, EX, RED, RAL, UBE

Answers to Letter Combinations

Q1. guz, zli, ng (guzzling)

Q2. juv, en, ile (juvenile)

Q3. ma, jes, tic (majestic)

Q4. adj, ust, ing (adjusting)

Q5. tra, nsp, ose (transpose)

Q6. buo, ya, nt (buoyant)

Q7. ce, rem, ony (ceremony)

Q8. do, min, ant (dominant)

Q9. pa, ral, lel (parallel)

Q10. wit, hdr, awn (withdrawn)

Q11. to, uri, st (tourist)

Q12. sti, let, to (stiletto)

Q13. jac, kha, mm, er (jackhammer)

Q14. mo, zza, rel, la (mozzarella)

Q15. xe, nop, hob, ia (xenophobia)

Q16. ac, qui, es, ce (acquiesce)

Q17. acc, om, pl, ice (accomplice)

Q18. jug, ger, na, ut (juggernaut)

Q19. adj, ou, rn (adjourn)

Q20. ex, ube, ra, nce (exuberance)

Sentence Structure

Question 1. Which two words need to be swapped around in order for the sentence to read correctly?

Doctors advise us to ensure the recommended amount of fruit and vegetables to eat a healthier lifestyle.

/

Question 2. Which two words need to be swapped around in order for the sentence to read correctly?

The elderly like to reminisce about their alive to not only make conversation but also keep their memories past.

/

Question 3. Which two words need to be swapped around in order for the sentence to read correctly?

Doctors are sometimes confused as to why a treatment is not following and it is often the case that the patient is not working their advice.

/

Question 4. Which two words need to be swapped around in order for the sentence to read correctly?

The men and women of the UK Fire Service carry out an amazing job. They are there to protect the pride in which they serve, and they do that job with great community, passion and very high levels of professionalism and commitment.

/

Question 5. Which two words need to be swapped around in order for the sentence to read correctly?

The post holder will work as part of a team to provide a safe, effective, efficient care environment for patients, relatives and carers. They will be supervision for the assessment, planning, implementation and evaluation of programmes of care under indirect responsible from senior staff.

/

Question 6. Which two words need to be swapped around in order for the sentence to read correctly?

The only way to maintain a low economy is to ensure that unemployment is strong and productivity is high.

/

Question 7. Which two words need to be swapped around in order for the sentence to read correctly?

The torrential rain had been flood down for 6 hours now, and the drain was beginning to pouring.

/

Question 8. Which two words need to be swapped around in order for the sentence to read correctly?

Danielle had left the gate open, presence in the neighbour's dog's resulting in the back garden.

/

Question 9. Which two words need to be swapped around in order for the sentence to read correctly?

If there was any consolation, it was that Eric would get to stay at home for the rest of the relax and week.

/

Question 10. Which two words need to be swapped around in order for the sentence to read correctly?

After correctly fitting their abseiling, the harnesses team began their descent of the mountain.

/

Question 11. Which two words need to be swapped around in order for the sentence to read correctly?

Emboldened by the pushed crowd, the athlete cheering herself to the absolute limit and made it to the finish line.

/

Question 12. Which two words need to be swapped around in order for the sentence to read correctly?

Given that the conditions were needed, the group worsening to decide whether to hunker down for a week or head out in the snow.

/

Question 13. Which two words need to be swapped around in order for the sentence to read correctly?

Ray had been so busy forgotten for his holiday that he had packing to pay for travel insurance.

/

Question 14. Which two words need to be swapped around in order for the sentence to read correctly?

The address on the letter was received, and so Michaela never incorrect the notification of her renewed parking permit.

/

Question 15. Which two words need to be swapped around in order for the sentence to read correctly?

The nest in the tree was getting impressive by the day, and was starting to look very bigger.

/

Answers to Sentence Structure

Q1. ensure / eat

Doctors advise us to **eat** the recommended amount of fruit and vegetables to **ensure** a healthier lifestyle.

Q2. alive / past

The elderly like to reminisce about their **past** to not only make conversation but also keep their memories **alive**.

Q3. following / working

Doctors are sometimes confused as to why a treatment is not **working** and it is often the case that the patient is not **following** their advice.

Q4. pride / community

The men and women of the UK Fire Service carry out an amazing job. They are there to protect the **community** in which they serve, and they do that job with great **pride**, passion and very high levels of professionalism and commitment.

Q5. supervision / responsible

The post holder will work as part of a team to provide a safe, effective, efficient care environment for patients, relatives and carers. They will be **responsible** for the assessment, planning, implementation and evaluation of programmes of care under indirect **supervision** from senior staff.

Q6. low / strong

The only way to maintain a **strong** economy is to ensure that unemployment is **low** and productivity is high.

Q7. flood / pouring

The torrential rain had been **pouring** down for 6 hours now, and the drain was beginning to **flood**.

Q8. presence / resulting

Danielle had left the gate open, **resulting** in the neighbour's dog's **presence** in the back garden.

Q9. relax / week

If there was any consolation, it was that Eric would get to stay at home for the rest of the **week** and **relax**.

Q10. abseiling / harnesses

After correctly fitting their **harnesses**, the **abseiling** team began their descent of the mountain.

Q11. pushed / cheering

Emboldened by the **cheering** crowd, the athlete **pushed** herself to the absolute limit and made it to the finish line.

Q12. needed / worsening

Given that the conditions were **worsening**, the group **needed** to decide whether to hunker down for a week or head out in the snow.

Q13. forgotten / packing

Ray had been so busy **packing** for his holiday that he had **forgotten** to pay for travel insurance.

Q14. received / incorrect

The address on the letter was **incorrect**, and so Michaela never **received** the notification of her renewed parking permit.

Q15. impressive / bigger

The nest in the tree was getting **bigger** by the day, and was starting to look very **impressive**.

Word Meanings

Question 1. Which of the following words is used to describe something that cannot be identified as different or distinct? Circle your answer.

A	B	C	D
Indistinguishable	Undescribable	Counterfeit	Differential

Question 2. Which of the following words is used to describe something that is closely associated with or suggestive of something? Circle your answer.

A	B	C	D
Unrelatable	Associatative	Related	Relinquishable

Question 3. Which of the following words is used to describe something that is equivalent in seriousness to, or virtually the same as? Circle your answer.

A	B	C	D
Punishable	Penetrative	Relinquishable	Tantamount

Question 4. Which of the following words is used to describe exaggerated statements or claims not meant to be taken literally? Circle your answer.

A	B	C	D
Effervescent	Hyperbole	Bullish	Deceitful

Question 5. Which of the following words is used to describe something that is corresponding in size or degree, in proportion? Circle your answer.

A	B	C	D
Parallel	Universal	Relatable	Commensurate

Question 6. Which of the following words describes something that is delicate and lightweight, in an otherworldly way? Circle your answer.

A	B	C	D
Corporeal	Ethereal	Bewildered	Celestial

Question 7. Which of the following words describes something that is not deterred by the possibility of danger, pain or death? Circle your answer.

A	B	C	D
Courageous	Captivated	Berserk	Belittled

Question 8. Which of the following words describes something that is untidy or poorly-kept? Circle your answer.

A	B	C	D
Crumpled	Marinated	Dishevelled	Bemused

Question 9. Which of the following words describes something that is convincing or believable? Circle your answer.

A	B	C	D
Presumptuous	Incredible	Assumptive	Credible

Question 10. Which of the following words describes something that is kept or done in secret? Circle your answer.

A	B	C	D
Berate	Clandestine	Blasphemous	Precociously

Question 11. Which of the following words describes something that is excessively severe? Circle your answer.

A	B	C	D
Embattled	Defective	Draconian	Capricious

Question 12. Which of the following words describes two things that are occurring at the same time, or in a similar way? Circle your answer.

A	B	C	D
Parallel	Inclination	Downfall	Causation

Question 13. Which of the following words describes a secret plan to commit something that is illegal or dangerous? Circle your answer.

A	B	C	D
Speculation	Deify	Decode	Conspiracy

Question 14. Which of the following words describes a comparison between two or more things using examples? Circle your answer.

A	B	C	D
Milquetoast	Boisterous	Analogy	Juxtaposition

Question 15. Which of the following words describes giving something a lot of public attention? Circle your answer.

A	B	C	D
Uninformed	Lionise	Behold	Interrogate

Answers to Letter Combinations

Q1. A = Indistinguishable

Q2. C = Related

Q3. D = Tantamount

Q4. B = Hyperbole

Q5. D = Commensurate

Q6. B = Ethereal

Q7. A = Courageous

Q8. C = Dishevelled

Q9. D = Credible

Q10. B = Clandestine

Q11. C = Draconian

Q12. A = Parallel

Q13. D = Conspiracy

Q14. C = Analogy

Q15. B = Lionise

Insert the Letter

Question 1. Which one letter will finish the word and begin the second word in each set? Circle your answer.

Bal (?) int   Cal (?) ild

M   D   T   K

Question 2. Which one letter will finish the word and begin the second word in each set? Circle your answer.

Wor (?) ale   Wal (?) nit

N   K   B   T

Question 3. Which one letter will finish the word and begin the second word in each set? Circle your answer.

Bul (?) ook   Tom (?) ull

T   E   B   N

Question 4. Which one letter will finish the word and begin the second word in each set? Circle your answer.

Tol (?) olt   Hol (?) oor

D   H   N   U

Question 5. Which one letter will finish the word and begin the second word in each set? Circle your answer.

Bur (?) orm   Tur (?) ile

T   N   B   U

Question 6. Which one letter will finish the word and begin the second word in each set? Circle your answer.

Bol (?) art   Hol (?) eal

I   N   B   D

Question 7. Which one letter will finish the word and begin the second word in each set? Circle your answer.

Bar (?) arn   Har (?) ach

N   E   F   T

Question 8. Which one letter will finish the word and begin the second word in each set? Circle your answer.

Hoo (?) ulp   Gul (?) ond

D   P   T   A

Question 9. Which one letter will finish the word and begin the second word in each set? Circle your answer.

Mel (?) ire   Fol (?) irt

T   D   E   Y

Question 10. Which one letter will finish the word and begin the second word in each set? Circle your answer.

Gur (?) gly   Men (?) ndo

Y   R   U   B

Question 11. Which one letter will finish the word and begin the second word in each set? Circle your answer.

Mak (?) ars   Mar (?) nvy

B   E   I   R

Question 12. Which one letter will finish the word and begin the second word in each set? Circle your answer.

Bee (?) ear   Cur (?) old

T   D   Y   N

Question 13. Which one letter will finish the word and begin the second word in each set? Circle your answer.

Ren (?) eal   Gol (?) ial

E   D   H   A

Question 14. Which one letter will finish the word and begin the second word in each set? Circle your answer.

Bac (?) ick   Bar (?) iss

E   P   K   T

Question 15. Which one letter will finish the word and begin the second word in each set? Circle your answer.

Hal (?) ome   Sal (?) rip

P   D   E   T

Answers to Insert the Letter

Q1. M

Balm and Mint, Calm and Mild

Q2. K

Work and Kale, Walk and Knit

Q3. B

Bulb and Book, Tomb and Bull

Q4. D

Told and Dolt, Hold and Door

Q5. N

Burn and Norm, Turn and Nile

Q6. D

Bold and Dart, Hold and Deal

Q7. E

Bare and Earn, Hare and Each

Q8. P

Hoop and Pulp, Gulp and Pond

Q9. D

Meld and Dire, Fold and Dirt

Q10. U

Guru and Ugly, Menu and Undo

Q11. E

Make and Ears, Mare and Envy

Q12. T

Beet and Tear, Curt and Told

Q13. D

Explanation = Rend and Deal, Gold and Dial

Q14. K

Back and Kick, Bark and Kiss

Q15. T

Halt and Tome, Salt and Trip

Move the Letter

Question 1. Which one letter can be moved from the first word to the second word to create two new words?

Pail   Pan

Question 2. Which one letter can be moved from the first word to the second word to create two new words?

Dice   Own

Question 3. Which one letter can be moved from the first word to the second word to create two new words?

Golden   Room

Question 4. Which one letter can be moved from the first word to the second word to create two new words?

Demon   Ever

Question 5. Which one letter can be moved from the first word to the second word to create two new words?

Grown   Gave

Question 6. Which one letter can be moved from the first word to the second word to create two new words?

Send   Mite

Question 7. Which one letter can be moved from the first word to the second word to create two new words?

Descent   Liver

Question 8. Which one letter can be moved from the first word to the second word to create two new words?

String Cow

Question 9. Which one letter can be moved from the first word to the second word to create two new words?

Bold Rain

Question 10. Which one letter can be moved from the first word to the second word to create two new words?

Praying Moon

Question 11. Which one letter can be moved from the first word to the second word to create two new words?

Burly Pie

Question 12. Which one letter can be moved from the first word to the second word to create two new words?

Learn East

Question 13. Which one letter can be moved from the first word to the second word to create two new words?

Provided Ash

Question 14. Which one letter can be moved from the first word to the second word to create two new words?

Smash Ham

Question 15. Which one letter can be moved from the first word to the second word to create two new words?

Dealt Meal

Answers to Move the Letter

Q1. I

Pal / Pain

Q2. D

Ice / Down

Q3. G

Olden / Groom

Q4. N

Demo / Never

Q5. R

Gown / Grave

Q6. S

End / Smite

Q7. S

Decent / Sliver

Q8. R

Sting / Crow

Q9. B

Old / Brain

Q10. R

Paying / Moron

Q11. L

Bury / Pile

Q12. L

Earn / Least

Q13. D

Provide / Dash

Q14. S

Mash / Sham

Q15. T

Deal / Metal

Word Fusion

Question 1. Which two words (one from each bracket) can be combined to create a new word?

(care cook kind) (full less hold)

Question 2. Which two words (one from each bracket) can be combined to create a new word?

(taste motor tell) (way guide petrol)

Question 3. Which two words (one from each bracket) can be combined to create a new word?

(bow light brain) (call man irate)

Question 4. Which two words (one from each bracket) can be combined to create a new word?

(sea rabbit fleet) (pull horse lion)

Question 5. Which two words (one from each bracket) can be combined to create a new word?

(grave hay husband) (animal yard ham)

Question 6. Which two words (one from each bracket) can be combined to create a new word?

(shadow feather signal) (axe boxing wave)

Question 7. Which two words (one from each bracket) can be combined to create a new word?

(god tail free) (fall top brave)

Question 8. Which two words (one from each bracket) can be combined to create a new word?

(cool prior tame) (breath ant pea)

Question 9. Which two words (one from each bracket) can be combined to create a new word?

(bile black mucous) (out ice dale)

Question 10. Which two words (one from each bracket) can be combined to create a new word?

(tyre camp pack) (site tile terrible)

Question 11. Which two words (one from each bracket) can be combined to create a new word?

(coal berate shoe) (entry lace box)

Question 12. Which two words (one from each bracket) can be combined to create a new word?

(over under between) (tell told come)

Question 13. Which two words (one from each bracket) can be combined to create a new word?

(court crow kind) (box told room)

Question 14. Which two words (one from each bracket) can be combined to create a new word?

(god tap tickle) (brake speed hand)

Question 15. Which two words (one from each bracket) can be combined to create a new word?

(trap blow bend) (out mend made)

Answers to Word Fusion

Q1. care/less

Careless

Q2. motor/way

Motorway

Q3. bow/man

Bowman

Q4. sea/horse

Seahorse

Q5. grave/yard

Graveyard

Q6. shadow/boxing

Shadowboxing

Q7. free/fall

Freefall

Q8. cool/ant

Coolant

Q9. black/out

Blackout

Q10. camp/site

Campsite

Q11. shoe/lace

Shoelace

Q12. over/come

Overcome

Q13. court/room

Courtroom

Q14. god/speed

Godspeed

Q15. blow/out

Blowout

Word Meanings

Question 1. Which word fits in both sets of brackets? Circle your answer.

(Unsympathetic, Blunt) (Winter, Snow)

Cold   Hot   Brown   Snail

Question 2. Which word fits in both sets of brackets? Circle your answer.

(Wave, Swim) (Fish, Shark)

Pond   Hand   Sea   Foot

Question 3. Which word fits in both sets of brackets? Circle your answer.

(Punch, Fist) (Bowling, Baseball)

Tuna   Strike   Catfish   Cheese

Question 4. Which word fits in both sets of brackets? Circle your answer.

(Basin, Cutlery) (Drown, Dive)

Ocean   Cat   Sink   Tennis

Question 5. Which word fits in both sets of brackets? Circle your answer.

(Fake, Pretend) (Penicillin, Injection)

Grass   Pen   Ballpoint   Doctor

Question 6. Which word fits in both sets of brackets? Circle your answer.

(Power, Watt) (Ram, Assault)

Punching   Kicking   Battery   Boxing

Question 7. Which word fits in both sets of brackets? Circle your answer.

(Verdict, Decision) (Write, Grammar)

Punctuate   Sentence   Destroy   Annihilate

Question 8. Which word fits in both sets of brackets? Circle your answer.

(Safe, Steady) (Hay, Jodhpurs)

Chickens   Stable   Farm   Sky

Question 9. Which word fits in both sets of brackets? Circle your answer.

(Iris, Retina) (Study, Learn)

Soldier   Ballad   Retriever   Pupil

Question 10. Which word fits in both sets of brackets? Circle your answer.

(Birth, Appear) (Scheme, Plan)

Basket   Uterus   Cauliflower   Hatch

Question 11. Which word fits in both sets of brackets? Circle your answer.

(Excess, Superfluous) (Save, Mercy)

Murder   Grin   Carpet   Spare

Question 12. Which word fits in both sets of brackets? Circle your answer.

(Combine, Merge) (Dive, Float)

Lake   Pool   Gasp   Sigh

Question 13. Which word fits in both sets of brackets? Circle your answer.

(Chase, Tease) (Perform, Act)

Play   Movie   Library   Shout

Question 14. Which word fits in both sets of brackets? Circle your answer.

(Spell, Cast) (Professional, Teacher)

Wand   Sword   Handgun   Staff

Question 15. Which word fits in both sets of brackets? Circle your answer.

(Plan, Template) (Select, Pick)

Draft   Delete   Terminate   Show

Answers to Word Meanings

Q1. Cold

If someone is unsympathetic or blunt they could also be seen as acting in a cold manner. Likewise, 'winter' and 'snow' are both associated with cold, in terms of weather.

Q2. Sea

Waves and swimming are associated with the sea. The sea is also where you will find fish and sharks.

Q3. Strike

Both punch and fist are closely associated with striking someone. In bowling, players aim to score a strike. In baseball, the players are given three chances, or strikes.

Q4. Sink

A basin is also known as a sink, and a sink is where you wash up cutlery. Sinking is also commonly associated with drowning, and diving into water.

Q5. Doctor

The term doctor is not just a name given for a medical professional, which links with penicillin and injections. Doctor is another word for committing fraudulent activity.

Q6. Battery

The terms power and watt are associated with electricity, which links with batteries – used to supply power to electronic devices. Battery is also the name for a violent action, such as assault, or ramming something.

Q7. Sentence

To sentence someone, in legal terms, is to reach a decision or verdict on their legal status. Writing and grammar are also associated with literary sentences.

Q8. Stable

The term stable can mean safe or steady, i.e. in a fixed or balanced manner. It is also the name for a horse's home, in which you will find hay, and jodhpurs (riding boots).

Q9. Pupil

The pupil forms a part of the eye, as does the iris and the retina. Likewise, pupils at school study and learn.

Q10. Hatch

Hatching, in animals born from eggs, relates to birth and the time when they first appear in the world. Hatch can also mean to scheme or plan, for example, 'I hatched a clever plan.'

Q11. Spare

Excess or superfluous relate to 'having too much', or spare. The term spare is also used to describe the act of 'refraining from harming someone'.

Q12. Pool

The terms combine and merge can refer to 'pooling' something together, or adding things to one group. Likewise, you would dive or float in a (swimming) pool.

Q13. Play

Chasing or teasing are both acts associated with playing. In a dramatic play, actors perform or act.

Q14. Staff

In fantastical terms, a staff is used to cast spells. A professional person, or a teacher, could be considered a member of staff.

Q15. Draft

A template or plan is a term used for an early form of work, which is missing something (the same as a draft). In sports, a draft is where players are selected or picked.

Comprehension

Read the following passage and answer the questions as either TRUE, FALSE or IMPOSSIBLE TO SAY based on the information provided.

Speaker 1. Grammar provides the structure upon which all writing is built. Without grammar, the world would fall into chaos. Life as we know it would plunge into abject mediocrity. One can only imagine the catastrophe that would befall the world without the invention of grammar. Commands from generals in the battlefield would be mistranslated. Public transport would be utterly disrupted. I can't imagine a world without grammar, and I'm not sure I want to.

Speaker 2. Some people are extremely uppity about grammar. I'm not that bothered by it. The main thing for me, when reading a book, is that I can understand what is being said. I appreciate that grammar is particularly useful, and can help to distinguish between certain types of phrases and words when used correctly, but for the most part I can get along just fine without precise or perfect grammar. That being said, I appreciate that grammar makes a big impact on the world we live in, and that when it comes to public affairs it can make a big difference to the way things are perceived. Grammar matters, just not as much as people think it does.

Question 1. Speaker 1 believes that public transport would suffer, if grammar did not exist.

| True | | False | | Impossible to say |

Question 2. Speaker 2 believes that grammar has no impact upon the outcome of wars and battles.

| True | | False | | Impossible to say |

Question 3. The two speakers agree that grammar has a sustained impact on public life.

| True | | False | | Impossible to say |

Question 4. The idea of a world without grammar, is too distressing for speaker 1 to think about.

| True | | False | | Impossible to say |

Question 5. Speaker 2 regards the relatability of a book as being more important than the use of grammar.

| True | | False | | Impossible to say |

Read the following passage and answer the questions as either TRUE, FALSE or IMPOSSIBLE TO SAY based on the information provided.

As vegetarianism, and indeed veganism, becomes more and more popular, people who don't fit into either of these two groups are facing a growing moral conundrum. Do they continue as they are, knowing the facts about the meat industry, or do they take steps to make a positive, moral change?

While it might seem easy for a person who has been brought up as a vegetarian to point the finger, the bottom line is that it's not that simple. It's a significant change to one's diet, not just a simple one-step process. From the beginning of time, humans have been conditioned to consume meat, and therefore by breaking this diet we are breaking from hundreds of thousands of years of mental conditioning. Some people have the willpower, and the moral fortitude, to do this, and more power to them. Others, including myself, are not so strong.

That being said, it's almost undeniable at this point that living as a meat eater, is to confront, or wilfully ignore in this case, your own hypocrisy. We look upon the perpetrators of these acts with dismay, whilst wilfully consuming pigs, chickens, and cows which have been raised for slaughter. We attend the zoo, knowing in the back of our minds that it's not right to cage animals in this way. Are we really any better than the people perpetrating these awful acts?

Question 6. The narrator is a meat eater.

True | False | Impossible to say

Question 7. The narrator believes that breaking our mental conditioning is solely down to the strength of our willpower.

True | False | Impossible to say

Question 8. According to the passage, attending the zoo is a hypocritical act.

True | False | Impossible to say

Question 9. Based on the passage, the narrator believes that it's more acceptable to eat animals which have been raised for slaughter, than wild animals.

True | False | Impossible to say

Question 10. The writer believes that adopting vegetarianism or veganism, is a moral move.

True | False | Impossible to say

Read the following passage and answer the questions as either TRUE, FALSE or IMPOSSIBLE TO SAY based on the information provided.

> If you've ever worked in a customer service role, you'll be aware of the challenges that such a position brings. This is even more so when it comes to the various forms of communication. If a customer approaches you in person, then you can generally expect that they'll be a bit more polite. Of course, this isn't always the case, but in Britain especially we are not particularly confrontational. As a whole, we don't like to get into big shouting matches, especially in front of others. Via email, it's a completely different story. If you're dealing with angry customers via email, then you can be assured they won't hold back. Below is one such typical example:
>
> Hi there,
>
> I DEMAND a refund from your company. I've been signed up for this gym membership for 1 month now, and I haven't even lost a single stone. Refund me IMMEDIATELY or I will escalate this situation further, calling in the police and the armed forces. I repeat, YOU WILL refund me, or there will be consequences.
>
> I look forward to hearing from you,
>
> Kevin.
>
> The saying 'treat others as you would like to be treated' has become a cliché, but it's certainly true. There's just no need to be rude, especially if you want someone to help you.

Question 11. Kevin received a refund from the company.

True | False | Impossible to say

Question 12. The writer believes that if you want people to be nice to you, then you should be nice to them.

True | False | Impossible to say

Question 13. The writer believes that people are more confrontational via email.

True | False | Impossible to say

Question 14. The writer feels that British people will try to avoid face-to-face arguments.

True | False | Impossible to say

Question 15. When working in a customer service role, you may have to deal with unhappy customers.

True | False | Impossible to say

Read the following passage and answer the questions as either TRUE, FALSE or IMPOSSIBLE TO SAY based on the information provided.

In the wake of Lenin's death, a power struggle emerged within the Bolshevik party of the Soviet Union. On the one side, was Joseph Stalin. On the other side, Leon Trotsky. As it happened, Stalin astutely outmanoeuvred Trotsky, and the latter was exiled from the country.

On the face of it, it is quite shocking that Trotsky failed. Here was an astute politician (widely regarded as far more intelligent than Stalin) who had been personally recommended as the next leader by Lenin's testament. Yet, there are several reasons why success did not follow. Firstly, the testament of Lenin was hidden by Stalin and other members of the party. The letter (although excusing them) drew attention to Kamenev and Zinoviev's doubts over the 1917 revolution, and thus it was beneficial for them to aid Stalin in covering this up. This was compounded by Trotsky's notoriously prickly and over-confident nature, which riled the other members of the Politburo.

Trotsky's own ideology posed another problem. Trotsky wanted to expand the socialist revolution throughout the world, and cause an international uprising. Stalin used Trotsky's ideas against him, claiming that they were a threat to the nation.

By 1940, Trotsky was dead – exiled and assassinated at Stalin's command. With nobody left to oppose him, Joseph Vissarionovich had won.

Question 16. Trotsky died in 1940.

True | False | Impossible to say

Question 17. Stalin had doubts about the 1917 revolution.

True | False | Impossible to say

Question 18. Lenin recommended that Trotsky shouldn't succeed him as leader of the party.

True | False | Impossible to say

Question 19. Kamenev and Zinoviev were members of the NKVD.

True | False | Impossible to say

Question 20. The other members of the Politburo got along with Trotsky.

True | False | Impossible to say

Read the following passage and answer the questions as either TRUE, FALSE or IMPOSSIBLE TO SAY based on the information provided.

> Amongst academics and humanities students, you'll often find that there is a clear split in opinion on the validity of creative writing as a taught subject.
>
> Non-believers claim that the problem isn't with the subject itself, it's with the way that lecturers are naturally inclined to teach it. Creative writing lessons, they say, simply become a way for lecturers to turn students into a pastiche of themselves, with little to no direction of their own.
>
> Then, there is the marking system itself. Can you really grade a piece of writing from 1-100? Written fiction is not the same as an essay, it is subjective, and to assign a score from 1-100 or even a grade (for example Pass, Merit, Distinction) seems utterly benign.
>
> Now, most students simply produce stylistically carbon copies of their lecturers own writing; rather than focusing on their own work. Naturally those who don't conform then receive lower marks, while egotistical lecturers are more than happy to give out higher grades to those who replicate said lecturer's own work, attend extra-curricular events, or meet up at the pub after classes.

Question 21. The writer believes that students receive higher marks from their lecturers, if they replicate said lecturer's writing style.

True | False | Impossible to say

Question 22. According to the passage, there is no point in grading fiction, or assigning it a score.

True | False | Impossible to say

Question 23. Students and academics are split on whether creative writing can really be taught.

True | False | Impossible to say

Question 24. According to the passage, meeting with your lecturers at the pub after classes, will not improve your grade.

True | False | Impossible to say

Question 25. The writer believes that Creative Writing should not be taught as a degree.

True | False | Impossible to say

Read the following passage and answer the questions as either TRUE, FALSE or IMPOSSIBLE TO SAY based on the information provided.

> Homer's Odyssey tells the story of Odysseus's return home from the Trojan War. After undergoing many years' worth of trials and tribulations, Odysseus finally reaches his homeland and avenges the honour of his wife. Odysseus is a hero ...
>
> The above black and white reading is exactly the way that schools are teaching the subject, and it's wrong. We know that the stereotypical Ancient Greek male protagonist was a manly, brash and courageous individual; willing to fight to the death if necessary. Odysseus fits this stereotype almost perfectly. However, literature has evolved, times have changed. Odysseus is no hero.
>
> The Odyssey is fundamentally flawed in its portrayal of Odysseus as a hero. To look at the work in the same manner as the Greeks did is to encourage ignorance. Why do we treat Poseidon as the villain of the text, when Odysseus blinds Poseidon's son (and then boasts about it)? Why do we refer to Odysseus as 'resourceful' when in actual fact he is simply a liar (who lies to his friends and family too, and not just his enemies)? Why do we pretend that Odysseus deserves the respect of his wife, and why do we pretend that he is a great leader, when he sends his men out to die (whilst he sits on the ship)? Even the ending is flawed, in that Athena essentially cheats for Odysseus, who would surely die otherwise.
>
> It's time for a change. No longer should we look at Greek literature in the same ignorant manner. We have evolved, and so should our ability to think for ourselves.

Question 26. The writer believes that Odysseus is rightly portrayed as a hero.

| True | False | Impossible to say |

Question 27. The writer believes that people are reading Greek literature in an ignorant manner.

| True | False | Impossible to say |

Question 28. Odysseus blinds Poseidon's son.

| True | False | Impossible to say |

Question 29. The stereotypical Ancient Greek male protagonist was manly, brash and courageous.

| True | False | Impossible to say |

Question 30. The writer feels that the ending of the Odyssey is flawless.

| True | False | Impossible to say |

ANSWERS TO VERBAL COMPREHENSION TEST

Q1. True

Speaker 1 states, 'Public transport would be utterly disrupted.' Therefore, the answer is true.

Q2. Impossible To Say

Speaker 2 makes no reference to the impact that grammar has on wars and battles. Therefore, the answer is impossible to say.

Q3. True

Speaker 1 states, 'Public transport would be utterly disrupted.' Meanwhile, Speaker 2 states, 'I appreciate that grammar makes a big impact on the world we live in, and that when it comes to public affairs it can make a big difference to the way things are perceived.' This shows that both speakers believe grammar has a sustained impact on public life, and therefore the answer is true.

Q4. True

Speaker 1 states, 'I cannot imagine a world without grammar, and I'm not sure I want to.' Therefore, the answer is true.

Q5. Impossible To Say

While speaker 2 discusses the importance of being able to understand a book, he does not reference relatability, and therefore the answer is impossible to say.

Q6. True

The speaker states, 'Some people have the willpower, and the moral fortitude, to do this, and more power to them. Others, including myself, are not so strong.' This indicates that he/she is a meat eater, and therefore the answer is true.

Q7. False

The speaker states, 'We are breaking from hundreds of thousands of years of mental conditioning. Some people have the willpower, and the moral fortitude, to do this, and more power to them.' This shows the mental fortitude is another element that factors into breaking one's mental conditioning, meaning willpower is not the sole element. Therefore, the answer is false.

Q8. True

The speaker clearly correlates going to the zoo with hypocrisy: 'That being said, it's almost undeniable at this point that living as a meat eater, is to confront, or wilfully ignore in this case, your own hypocrisy …we attend the zoo, knowing in the back of our minds that it's not right to cage animals in this way.' Therefore, the answer is true.

Q9. Impossible To Say

The speaker does not give an opinion on whether it's more acceptable to eat animals raised for slaughter, than wild animals. He/she states, 'We look upon the perpetrators of these acts with dismay, whilst wilfully consuming pigs, chickens, and cows which have been raised for slaughter', but this does not tell us whether he/she thinks one is worse than the other. Therefore, the answer is impossible to say.

Q10. True

In the first paragraph, the speaker states, 'Do they continue as they are, knowing the facts about the meat industry, or do they take steps to make a positive, moral change?' When combined with the first line of the first paragraph, 'As vegetarianism, and indeed veganism, becomes more and more popular, people who don't fit into either of these two groups are facing a growing moral conundrum' we can see that the speaker is associating veganism and vegetarianism with morality.

Q11. Impossible To Say

The passage does not make reference as to whether Kevin actually received a refund. Therefore, the answer is impossible to say.

Q12. True

The passage states, 'The saying 'treat others as you would like to be treated' has become a cliché, but it's certainly true. There's just no need to be rude, especially if you want someone to help you.' Therefore, the answer is true.

Q13. True

The passage states, 'As a whole, we don't like to get into big shouting matches, especially in front of others. Via email, it's a completely different story.' Therefore, the answer is true.

Q14. True

The passage states, 'Of course, this isn't always the case, but in Britain especially we are not particularly confrontational. As a whole, we don't like to get into big shouting matches, especially in front of others.' Therefore, the answer is true.

Q15. True

We can see from the passage as a whole, that working in customer service may require you to deal with unhappy customers.

Q16. Impossible To Say

The passage states, 'By 1940, Trotsky was dead – exiled and assassinated at Stalin's command.' Therefore, based on the passage, we cannot say exactly when Trotsky died. Thus, the answer is impossible to say.

Q17. Impossible To Say

The passage makes reference to Kamenev and Zinoviev's doubts, not Stalin's. Based on the passage, we do not know how Stalin felt about the revolution. Therefore, the answer is impossible to say.

Q18. False

The passage states, 'On the face of it, it is quite shocking that Trotsky failed. Here was an astute politician (widely regarded as far more intelligent than Stalin) who had been personally recommended as the next leader by Lenin's testament.' This shows that Lenin did recommend Trotsky, and therefore the answer is false.

Q19. Impossible To Say

The passage makes no reference to whether Kamenev and Zinoviev were in the NKVD. Therefore, the answer is impossible to say.

Q20. False

The passage states, 'This was compounded by Trotsky's notoriously prickly and over-confident nature, which riled the other members of the Politburo.' This clearly indicates that the other members of the Politburo disliked Trotsky, and therefore the answer is false.

Q21. True

The passage states, 'Naturally those who don't conform then receive lower marks, while egotistical lecturers are more than happy to give out higher grades to those who replicate said lecturer's own work.' Therefore, the answer is true.

Q22. True

The passage states, '...to assign a score from 1-100 or even a grade (for example Pass, Merit, Distinction) seems utterly benign.' Therefore, the answer is true.

Q23. True

The passage states, '...you'll often find that there is a clear split in opinion on the validity of creative writing as a taught subject.' Therefore, the answer is true.

Q24. False

The passage states, 'Naturally those who don't conform then receive lower marks, while egotistical lecturers are more than happy to give out higher grades to those who … meet up at the pub after classes.' Therefore, the answer is false.

Q25. Impossible To Say

The passage is debating the validity of Creative Writing as a taught subject, but does not come to a conclusion as to whether it should be taught. Therefore, the answer is impossible to say.

Q26. False

The writer of the passage is clearly of the opinion that the portrayal of Odysseus as a hero, is incorrect. Therefore, the answer is false.

Q27. True

The passage states, 'I believe it's time for a change. No longer should we look at Greek literature in the same ignorant manner.' Therefore, the answer is true.

Q28. True

The passage states, 'Why do we treat Poseidon as the villain of the text, when Odysseus blinds Poseidon's son (and then boasts about it)?' Therefore, the answer is true.

Q29. True

The passage states, 'We know that the stereotypical Ancient Greek male protagonist was a manly, brash and courageous individual; willing to fight to the death if necessary.' Therefore, the answer is true.

Q30. False

The passage states, 'Even the ending is flawed, in that Athena essentially cheats for Odysseus, who would surely die otherwise.' Therefore, the answer is false.

Similar Words

Question 1. Identify which of the following sentences is correct. Circle your answer.

A) Harriet and James buried they're treasure in the back garden. No one would ever know.

B) Harriet and James buried their treasure in the back garden. No one would ever know.

C) Harriet and James berried their treasure in the back garden. No one would ever know.

D) Harriet and James buried their treasure in the back garden. No one would ever no.

Question 2. Identify which of the following sentences is correct. Circle your answer.

A) James needed money, and fast. He headed too the casino. Little did he know, he would loose everything.

B) James needed money, and fast. He headed to the casino. Little did he no, he would lose everything.

C) James needed money, and fast. He headed to the casino. Little did he know, he would lose everything.

D) James needed money, and fast. He headed too the casino. Little did he know, he would lose everything.

Question 3. Identify which of the following sentences is correct. Circle your answer.

A) 'How much further do we need to go?' Billy whined. 'It's not much further,' the man sighed, he was beginning to lose his patience.

B) 'How much farther do we need to go?' Billy whined. 'It's not much farther,' the man sighed, he was beginning to lose his patience.

C) 'How much further do we need to go?' Billy whined. 'It's not much farther,' the man sighed, he was beginning to lose his patience.

D) 'How much farther do we need to go?' Billy whined. 'It's not much further,' the man sighed, he was beginning to lose his patience.

Question 4. Identify which of the following sentences is correct. Circle your answer.

A) Since my wife left me, I have thought of nothing accept her.

B) Since my wife left me, I have thought of nothing except her.

C) Since my wife left me, I've thought of nothing accept her.

D) Since my wife left me, I've thought of nothing except hair.

Question 5. Identify which of the following sentences is correct. Circle your answer.

A) The man promised to send me the shoes I'd ordered. As I found out later, he'd lied.

B) The man promised to send me the shoes Id ordered. As I've found out later, he'd' lied.

C) The man promised to send me the shoes Id ordered. As I'd found out later, he'd lied.

D) The man promised to send me the shoes I'd ordered. As I've found out later, he'd lied.

Question 6. Identify which of the following sentences is correct. Circle your answer.

A) Undoubtedly the best breed of cat, is the Norwegian Forest Cat. They're tails are long and fluffy, and they've got enormous, curved claws.

B) Undoubtedly the best breed of cat, is the Norwegian Forest Cat. Their tails are long and fluffy, and theyve got enormous, curved claws.

C) Undoubtedly the best breed of cat, is the Norwegian Forest Cat. Their tails are long and fluffy, and they've got enormous, curved claws.

D) Undoubtedly the best breed of cat, is the Norwegian Forest Cat. They are tails are long and fluffy, and they've got enormous, curved claws.

Question 7. Identify which of the following sentences is correct. Circle your answer.

A) The man stared at my shoes. He pointed. 'What are you whereing!' he yelled.

B) The man stared at my shoes. He pointed. 'What are you wearing?' he yelled.

C) The man stared at my shoes. He pointed. 'What are you where?' he yelled.

D) The man stared at my shoes. He pointed. 'What are you wore?' he yelled.

Question 8. Identify which of the following sentences is correct. Circle your answer.

A) Were going to spend all of our time at the beach while the whether is nice.

B) We're going to spend all of are time at the beach while the weather is nice.

C) We're going to spend all of our time at the beach while the weather is nice.

D) We're going to spend all of are time at the beach while the weather is nice.

Question 9. Identify which of the following sentences is correct. Circle your answer.

A) I was asked to stay after school on Tuesday. The principle informed me that I had broken the school principals, and that he could not bear to keep me at the school.

B) I was asked to stay after school on Tuesday. The principle informed me that I had broken the school principles, and that he could not bear to keep me at the school.

C) I was asked to stay after school on Tuesday. The principal informed me that I had broken the school principals, and that he could not bear to keep me at the school.

D) I was asked to stay after school on Tuesday. The principal informed me that I had broken the school principles, and that he could not bear to keep me at the school.

Question 10. Identify which of the following sentences is correct. Circle your answer.

A) 'They're not ready to take the test,' the professor declared. 'None of them have done enough practise!'

B) 'Their not ready to take the test,' the professor declared. 'None of them have done enough practice.'

C) 'They are not ready to take the test,' the professor declared. 'None of them have done enough practice.'

D) 'They're not ready to take the test,' the professor declared. 'None of them have done enough practice.'

Question 11. Identify which of the following sentences is correct. Circle your answer.

A) The dentist asked me to lay down. Then the drilling began.

B) The dentist asked me to lie down. Then the drilling begun.

C) The dentist asked me to laid down. Then the drilling began.

D) The dentist asked me to lie down. Then the drilling began.

Question 12. Identify which of the following sentences is correct. Circle your answer.

A) My brother and I went on a picnic. It was a hot day, and we decided to jump in the lake. We stripped bear, and were just about to jump in the water, when there was a roar behind us. It was a bear. The bear chased us, bear, through the woods.

B) My brother and I went on a picnic. It was a hot day, and we decided to jump in the lake. We stripped bare, and were just about to jump in the water, when there was a roar behind us. It was a bear. The bear chased us, bare, through the woods.

C) My brother and I went on a picnic. It was a hot day, and we decided to jump in the lake. We stripped bare, and were just about to jump in the water, when there was a roar behind us. It was a bare. The bear chased us, bear, through the woods.

D) My brother and I went on a picnic. It was a hot day, and we decided to jump in the lake. We stripped bare, and were just about to jump in the water, when there was a roar behind us. It was a bear. The bare chased us, bare, through the woods.

Question 13. Identify which of the following sentences is correct. Circle your answer.

A) If you're standing in a stationary position, the snake wont bite you.

B) If your standing in a stationery position, the snake wont bite you.

C) If you're standing in a stationary position, the snake won't bite you.

D) If you're standing in a stationery position, the snake won't bite you.

Question 14. Identify which of the following sentences is correct. Circle your answer.

A) I was running out of patience with Luke. 'The way your going, there's no turning back.'

B) I was running out of patients with Luke. 'The way you're going, theres no turning back.'

C) I was running out of patience with Luke. 'The way you're going, there's no turning back.'

D) I was running out of patients with Luke. 'The way you're going, there's no turning back.'

Question 15. Identify which of the following sentences is correct. Circle your answer.

A) 'You will bring me the briefcase,' the man said. 'And you'll lay it at my feet.'

B) 'You'll bring me the briefcase,' the man said. 'And you'll lie it at my feet.'

C) 'You've bring me the briefcase,' the man said. 'And you'll lie it at my feet.'

D) 'You've bring me the briefcase,' the man said. 'And you'll lay it at my feet.'

Answers to Similar Words

Q1. B.

The term 'their' is used to indicate possession, in relation to people or things. The term 'they're' is a contraction for 'they are', which wouldn't make sense here.

Likewise, option B also uses the term 'know' correctly – which indicates knowledge. The term 'no' is used to indicate a negative.

Q2. C

C uses the words 'know', 'to' and 'lose' correctly. The term 'know' is used to indicate knowledge. The term 'to' is used to indicate a place that a person or thing is moving in the direction of. The term 'lose' is used to indicate that someone has misplaced something, or ceases to be in possession of said thing.

All of the other options use the term 'loose' – used to indicate that something is not firmly fixed in place, 'too' – used to indicate that something is being done in addition, or excess, or 'no' – which is used to indicate a negative.

Q3. B

The term 'farther' is used to identify a measurable period of time or distance. The term 'further' is used in reference to an immeasurable or metaphorical distance.

In this case, B is the only option which makes sense, since both Billy and the man are speaking in terms of physical distance.

Q4. B

The term 'except' is used to indicate an exception to the rule, or an anomaly. 'Accept' means to acknowledge or agree to/about something. Furthermore, this answer uses the term 'her' correctly, instead of 'hair'.

Q5. A

Answer option A is the only option which is grammatically correct. All the other sentences use contractions incorrectly. The term 'I'd' is a contraction for 'I had'. While option D uses this, it then uses the term 'I've' incorrectly, since this is an unnatural change of tense.

Q6. C

Option C uses the terms 'their' – in reference to plural ownership, and 'they've' which is a contraction of 'they have'

Q7. B

Option B is the only answer which spells the term 'wearing' correctly.

Q8. C

Option C is the only option which correctly uses 'we're', which is the correct contraction for 'we are', 'our' to indicate possession, and 'weather'. Were, are and whether are all incorrectly used in the other answer options.

Q9. D

Principal is the name for an education authority, or main idea. Principle is the name for a value or belief. Therefore, you cannot break the principal, nor can a principle physically inform you of something.

Q10. A

The term practise should be used, as it refers to the repetitive action of doing something many times over, with the aim of mastering it. Practise is a verb. The term 'practice' is a noun, and refers to 'the customary, habitual, or expected procedure or way of doing of something.' For example, 'I have recently opened a doctor's practice.'

Q11. D

The term 'lie' is used to refer to someone/something reclining. The term 'lay' describes the act of putting something down gently. Option D also uses the word 'began' correctly. Began is the past tense of begin.

Q12. B

A bear is a large and furry animal. Bare refers to a lack of something – in this case, clothing.

Q13. C

Option C is the only answer which correctly uses the terms 'stationary' – which refers to the act of standing completely still, and 'won't' – which is a contraction of 'will not'.

Q14. C

Option C is the only option which uses contractions 'you're' – short for 'you are' and 'there's' – short for 'there is', correctly. It also spells the term 'patience' in the correct way.

Q15. A

Option A is the only answer which uses both 'you'll' – a contraction of you will, and 'lay' correctly. In this case, 'lie' would be incorrect, as the term 'lay' refers to the action of putting or placing something down. Lie refers to the act of reclining.

Non-Verbal Reasoning

Non-Verbal Reasoning tests are often used to assess a person's ability to recognise shapes and patterns in regards to formations. The questions appear in diagrammatic and pictorial form, often referring to these tests as abstract or diagrammatic reasoning.

The importance of a Non-Verbal Reasoning test is to determine how well you can understand and visualise information to solve problems. You need to be able to recognise and identify patterns amongst abstract shapes and images.

Such tests may include:

- Determining identical shapes;
- Rotating shapes;
- Reflections of shapes;
- Finding the odd shape;
- Finding the missing shape;
- 3D shapes;
- Coding;
- Shading and colours;
- Number sequences.

All of these questions are likely to appear in a Non-Verbal Reasoning test. So, it is imperative that you get to grips with each question type and know how to answer them. This comprehensive guide will provide you with detailed examples of each of the question types, so you know what to expect in the testing sections. Also, we will provide you with detailed answers and explanations so you can check your answers at the end of each test and ensure you know how to reach the correct answer.

For psychometric testing, you need to aim for speed, as well as accuracy. It is important to be able to undergo these tests with the utmost confidence and composure, in order to work swiftly and efficiently through the questions.

Code Breakers

Work out the codes for the figures and decide which answer has the correct code for figure 4.

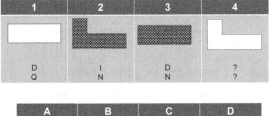

ANSWER = C (I, Q)

For the sample question above, you will notice that figures 1 and 3 both contain a rectangle. These rectangles are different colours, but the same size. This means that the code 'D' must represent the shape of a rectangle. You will notice that box 2 and 3 are of the same colour, but not the same shape. However, both have a code of 'N'. This code must represent the colour. To work out box 4, you need to find the code for both the shape and the colour. You already know that the shape of rectangles is coded 'D'. So, the code for the 'L' shape must be 'I'. (Box 2 has the code 'I' and 'N' and you have already worked out that 'N' is the code for the colour). Now you need to work out the colour. Box 1 has the same colour, and because you already know that code 'D' represents the rectangle shape, it leaves the code 'Q'.

Cube Nets

Work out which of the cubes can be made from the net.

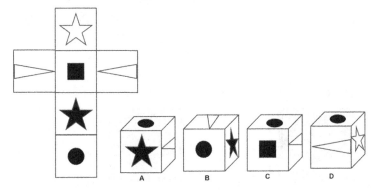

ANSWER = A

For these types of questions, you need to imagine that you are building a cube. The cube net has shapes on, so folding down the creases in order to make the cube, you need to work out where the shapes will be positioned. (Please note: these questions require you to fold the net so the shapes remain on the outside of the cube).

Sequences

Question 1. Which figure comes next in the sequence? Tick your answer.

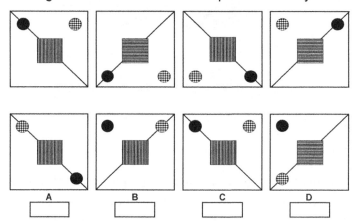

Question 2. Which figure comes next in the sequence? Tick your answer.

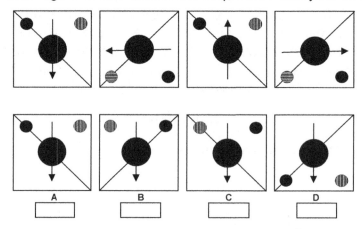

Question 3. Which figure comes next in the sequence? Tick your answer.

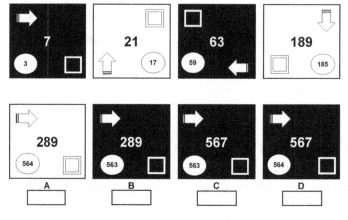

Question 4. Which figure comes next in the sequence? Tick your answer.

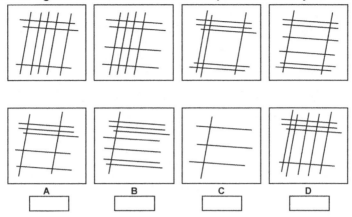

Question 5. Which figure comes next in the sequence? Tick your answer.

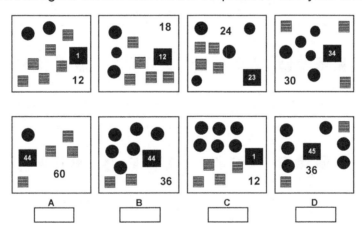

Question 6. Work out which option fits best in the missing square in order to complete the sequence. Tick your answer.

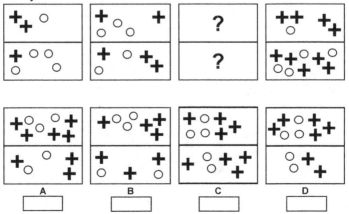

Question 7. Which figure comes next in the sequence? Tick your answer.

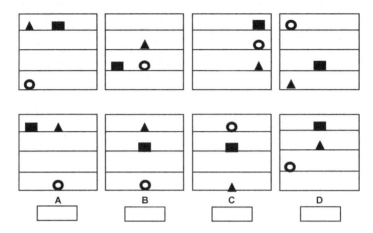

Question 8. Which figure comes next in the sequence? Tick your answer.

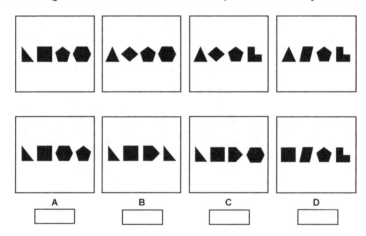

Question 9. Which figure comes next in the sequence? Tick your answer.

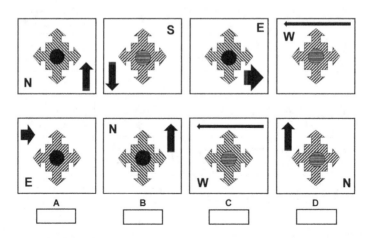

Question 10. Which figure comes next in the sequence? Tick your answer.

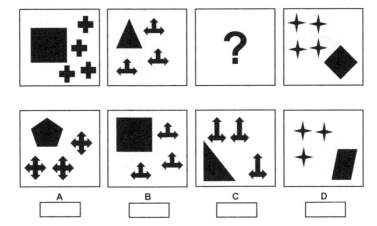

Question 11. Which figure comes next in the sequence? Tick your answer.

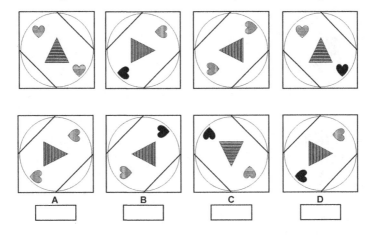

Question 12. Which figure comes next in the sequence? Tick your answer.

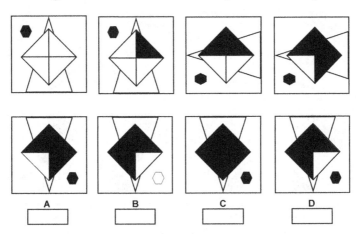

Question 13. Which figure comes next in the sequence? Tick your answer.

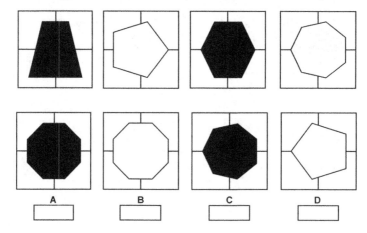

Question 14. Which figure comes next in the sequence? Tick your answer.

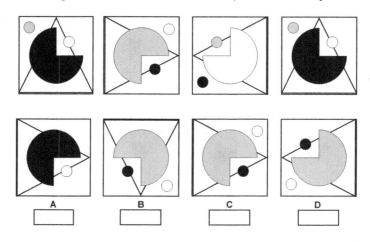

Question 15. Which figure comes next in the sequence? Tick your answer.

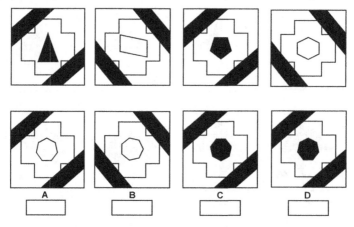

Answers to Sequences

Q1. C

→ The black circle is moving around the square anti-clockwise 90 degrees.

→ The patterned circle is moving around the square clockwise 90 degrees.

→ The black diagonal line alternates from top-left/bottom right to top-right/bottom left.

→ The internal, patterned square rotates 90 degrees each time.

Q2. A

→ The black circle alternates between top-left and bottom-right.

→ The patterned circle alternates between top-right and bottom-left and the lines alternate between horizontal and vertical.

→ The black diagonal line progresses 90 degrees clockwise in each square.

Q3. C

→ The main square alternates between black and white.

→ The arrow moves around the square anti-clockwise 90 degrees each time whilst also rotating itself anti-clockwise 90 degrees each time.

→ The square with the white border moves around the larger square anti-clockwise 90 degrees each time.

→ The internal number is multiplied by 3 each time. ($7 \times 3 = 21$; $21 \times 3 = 63$; $63 \times 3 = 189$; $189 \times 3 = 567$)

→ The white circle alternates between the bottom-left and bottom-right corner and is always 4 less than the number in the centre.

Q4. B

→ The number of vertical lines is decreasing by one each time and the number of horizontal lines is increasing by one each time.

Q5. D

→ The black circles are increasing by one each time.

→ The patterned squares are decreasing by one each time.

→ The number within the black square is increasing by 11 each time.

→ The number on its own is increasing by 6 each time.

Q6. B

→ Each square consists of two sections (top rectangle and bottom rectangle).

→ Starting at the top rectangle of the first square, the number of crosses and circles increases by one each time, moving from top rectangle to bottom rectangle as the sequence progresses.

→ Starting at the bottom rectangle of the first square, the number of crosses increases by one each time and the number of circles decreases by one each time, moving from bottom rectangle to top rectangle as the sequence progresses.

Q7. A

→ The black triangle moves down one level each time and one position to the right. Once it reaches the bottom, it goes back up to the top line.

→ The black rectangle moves down two levels each time and one position to the left. Once it reaches the bottom, it goes back up to the top line.

→ The circle moves up one level each time and one position to the right.

Q8. C

→ The number of sides on each shape, from left to right in each square, is 3, 4, 5 and 6 each time.

Q9. B

→ The main central shape stays the same; however, the lines within the shape switch from right to left and vice versa each time.

→ The central circle alternates from black to horizontal stripes each time.

→ The arrow within each square is pointing in the direction of the letter and goes from North, South, East, West each time.

Q10. C

→ The number of identical smaller shapes within each square is equal to the number of sides of each main shape.

Q11. C

→ The shape rotates 90 degrees clockwise, then flips 180 degrees.

→ The bottom-right heart changes from black to striped.

Q12. C

→ The square and its contents rotate 90 degrees anti-clockwise every other space in the sequence.

→ Then, another quadrant in the diamond changes from white to black.

Q13. A

→ The shape in the centre changes from black to white.

→ The shape gets an extra side each time (trapezium = 4 sides, pentagon = 5 sides, hexagon = 6 sides, and so on).

Q14. B

→ Both shapes rotates 90 degrees clockwise, then 180 degrees, then 90 degrees and so on

→ The shapes switch between black, grey, and white. Therefore, the answer must be a shape that has been rotated 180 degrees.

Q15. D

→ The entire shape rotates 180 degrees every time.

→ The centre shape changes from black to white and rotates 90 degrees.

→ The shape gains an extra side each time (triangle = 3 sides, parallelogram = 4 sides, pentagon = 5 sides, and so on).

Similar Shapes

Question 1. Which of the answer options is most like the question figures? Tick your answer.

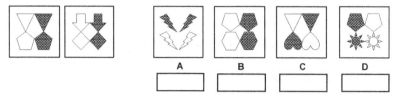

Question 2. Which of the answer options is most like the question figures? Tick your answer.

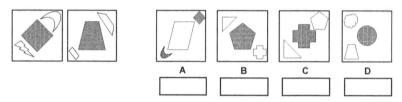

Question 3. Which of the answer options is most like the question figures? Tick your answer.

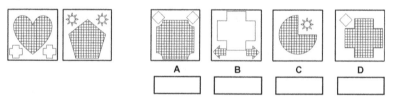

Question 4. Which of the answer options is most like the question figures? Tick your answer.

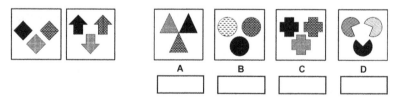

Question 5. Which of the answer options is most like the question figures? Tick your answer.

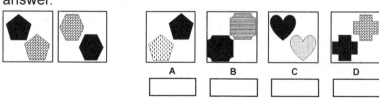

Question 6. Which of the answer options is most like the question figures? Tick your answer.

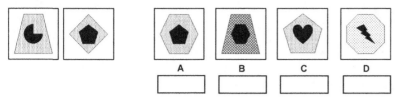

Question 7. Which of the answer options is most like the question figures? Tick your answer.

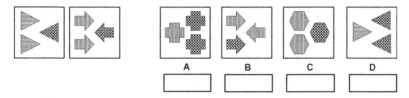

Question 8. Which of the answer options is most like the question figures? Tick your answer.

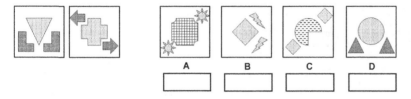

Question 9. Which of the answer options is most like the question figures? Tick your answer.

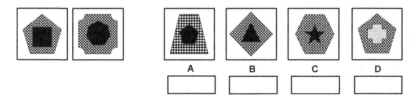

Question 10. Which of the answer options is most like the question figures? Tick your answer.

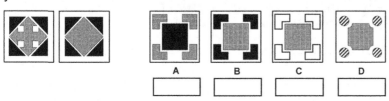

Question 11. Which of the answer options is most like the question figures? Tick your answer.

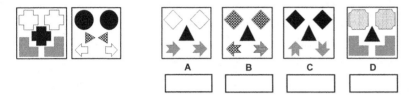

Question 12. Which of the answer options is most like the question figures? Tick your answer.

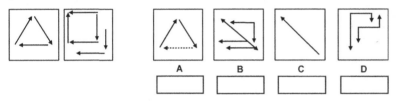

Question 13. Which of the answer options is most like the question figures? Tick your answer.

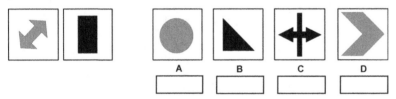

Question 14. Which of the answer options is most like the question figures? Tick your answer.

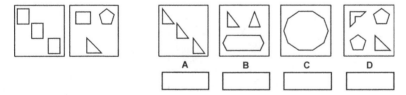

Question 15. Which of the answer options is most like the question figures? Tick your answer.

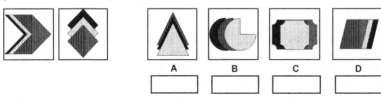

Answers to Similar Shapes

Q1. B

The two shapes on the left are white. The two shapes on the right have the 'brick' pattern.

Q2. C

The central shape has diagonal lines. It is accompanied by a shape at the bottom left, and a shape at the top right. Both of these shapes are white.

Q3. A

The central shape has a grid pattern. It is accompanied by a pair of identical smaller shapes. These are both white.

Q4. C

The left-hand shape is black. The right-hand shape has a 'brick' pattern. The bottom shape has diagonal lines.

Q5. D

There are two identical shapes. One is black, the other has a diagonal 'brick' pattern.

Q6. A

The larger shape has a dotted pattern. The smaller shape is black. The small shape has one less edge than the large shape.

Q7. C

The left-hand shapes have vertical stripes. The right-hand shape has a chequered pattern. There must be two shapes on the left and one shape on the right.

Q8. D

The middle shape has a dotted pattern. The two identical smaller shapes have diagonal stripes.

Q9. B

The larger shape has a chequered pattern. The smaller shape is black and must have one less edge than the large shape.

Q10. B

The central shape has diagonal stripes with a positive gradient. It is accompanied by four black shapes.

Q11. D

The question figures have a line of vertical symmetry.

Q12. C

Every arrow must consist of a single, solid straight line with one triangular point.

Q13. C

The shapes have two lines of symmetry.

Q14. B

The number of edges adds up to 12.

Q15. D

The shape at the back is black. The shape at the front has vertical stripes. The central shape has a dotted pattern.

Odd One Out

Question 1. Which answer figure is the odd one out? Tick your answer.

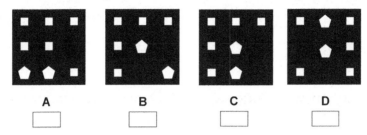

A	B	C	D

Question 2. Which answer figure is the odd one out? Tick your answer.

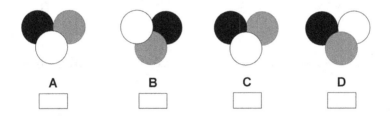

A	B	C	D

Question 3. Which answer figure is the odd one out? Tick your answer.

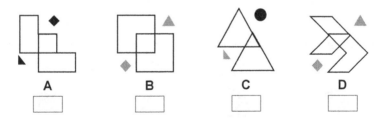

A	B	C	D

Question 4. Which answer figure is the odd one out? Tick your answer.

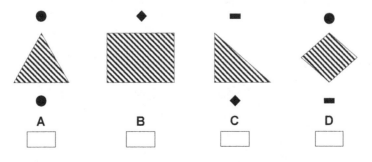

A	B	C	D

Question 5. Which answer figure is the odd one out? Tick your answer.

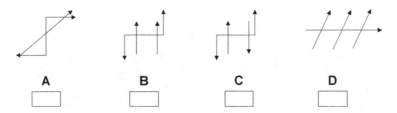

A	B	C	D

Question 6. Which answer figure is the odd one out? Tick your answer.

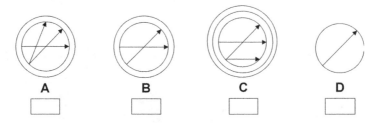

A	B	C	D

Question 7. Which answer figure is the odd one out? Tick your answer.

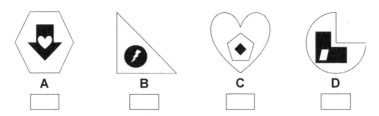

A	B	C	D

Question 8. Which answer figure is the odd one out? Tick your answer.

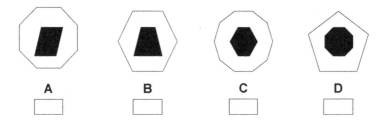

A	B	C	D

Question 9. Which answer figure is the odd one out? Tick your answer.

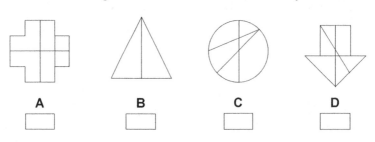

A	B	C	D

Question 10. Which answer figure is the odd one out? Tick your answer.

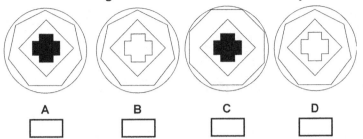

A	B	C	D

Question 11. Which answer figure is the odd one out? Tick your answer.

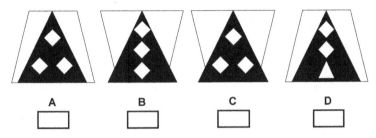

A	B	C	D

Question 12. Which answer figure is the odd one out? Tick your answer.

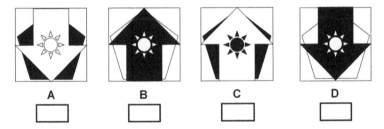

A	B	C	D

Question 13. Which answer figure is the odd one out? Tick your answer.

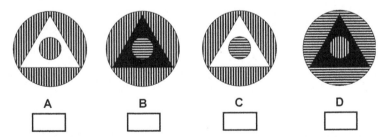

A	B	C	D

Question 14. Which answer figure is the odd one out? Tick your answer.

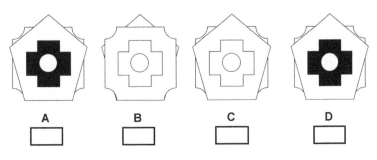

A	B	C	D

Question 15. Which answer figure is the odd one out? Tick your answer.

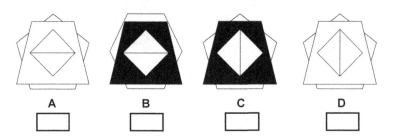

A

B

C

D

Answers to Odd One Out

Q1. A

All of the other figures contain five squares and two pentagons. Figure A contains six squares.

Q2. D

Figure B is the odd one out because all of the other figures have the white circle at the front. In Figure D, the white circle is in the background.

Q3. C

Figure C is the odd one out because all of the other figures contain two small shapes of the same colour. Figure C contains one small grey shape and one small black shape.

Q4. B

Figure B is the odd one out because it is missing a small shape underneath the large shape.

Q5. A

Figures B, C, and D all contain four arrow heads, whilst Figure A only has three arrow heads.

Q6. A

Figure A is the odd one out because the number of arrows does not match the number of rings. In Figures B, C, and D, the amount of arrows corresponds to the number of rings (2, 3, and 1, respectively). Figure A has three arrows, but only two rings. Therefore, A is the odd one out.

Q7. C

The colour of the shapes in each figure alternates as follows (from largest to smallest): white, black, white. The 'middle' shape in each figure is black, with the exception of Figure C, where the pattern is white, white, black. Therefore, Figure C is the odd one out.

Q8. D

Figures A, B, and C are all comprised of an external shape with an even number of sides, as well as an interior shape with an even number of sides. In Figure D, the exterior shape has five sides. Therefore, Figure D is the odd one out.

Q9. B

Figures A, C, and D contain three lines inside their shapes. Figure B only has one line within it, making it the odd one out.

Q10. C

The first shape inside the circle is an octagon, whilst in the other shapes it is a heptagon.

Q11. D

The bottom shape in the triangle, which should be a diamond, is also a triangle.

Q12. A

Figure A is the only option to not follow the pattern of alternating the colours of each shape (white, black, white or black, white, black).

Q13. A

The large and small circle both have a vertical stripe pattern. In all the other answer figures the small circle has the opposite strip pattern (vertical/horizontal) to the large circle.

Q14. B

The pentagon is at the back of the image, whilst it isn't in the other images.

Q15. B

The shape at the back of the image is a hexagon, whilst in the others it is a pentagon.

Rotate the Figure

Question 1. Which option is NOT a rotation of the question figure? Tick your answer

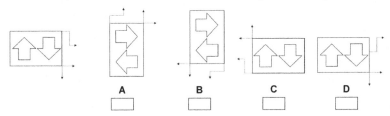

Question 2. Which option is NOT a rotation of the question figure? Tick your answer.

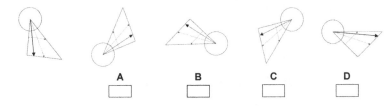

Question 3. Which option is NOT a rotation of the question figure? Tick your answer.

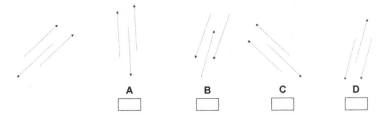

Question 4. Which option is NOT a rotation of the question figure? Tick your answer.

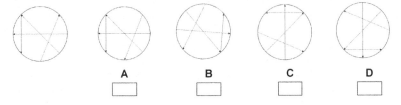

Question 5. Which option is NOT a rotation of the question figure? Tick your answer.

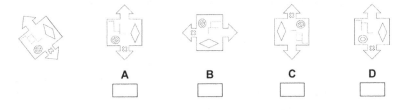

Question 6. Which option is NOT a rotation of the question figure? Tick your answer.

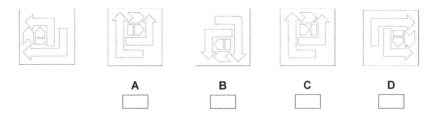

| A | B | C | D |

Question 7. Which option is NOT a rotation of the question figure? Tick your answer.

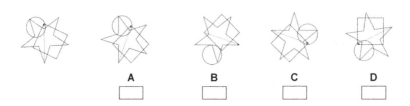

| A | B | C | D |

Question 8. Which option is NOT a rotation of the question figure? Tick your answer

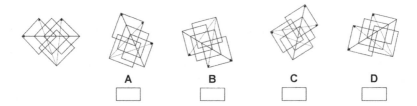

| A | B | C | D |

Question 9. Which option is NOT a rotation of the question figure? Tick your answer

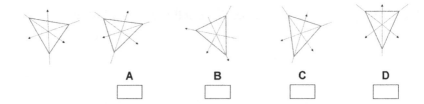

| A | B | C | D |

Question 10. Which option is NOT a rotation of the question figure? Tick your answer

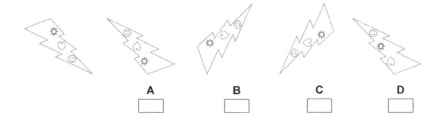

| A | B | C | D |

Question 11. Which option is NOT a rotation of the question figure? Tick your answer

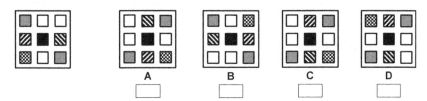

Question 12. Which option is NOT a rotation of the question figure? Tick your answer

Question 13. Which option is NOT a rotation of the question figure? Tick your answer

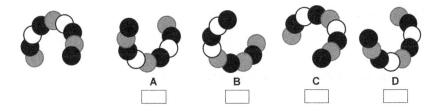

Question 14. Which option is NOT a rotation of the question figure? Tick your answer

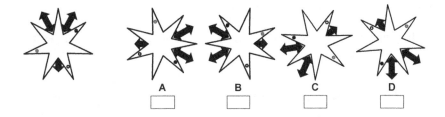

Question 15. Which option is NOT a rotation of the question figure? Tick your answer

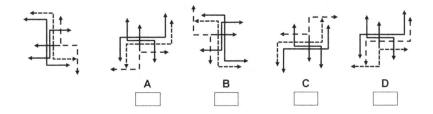

Answers to Rotate the Figure

Q1. D

The 'Z'-shaped arrow is flipped.

Q2. D

The big arrow on Figure D is pointing to the wrong corner of the triangle.

Q3. B

The direction of the arrows in figure B do not match the sample figure.

Q4. A

One of the arrows is pointing in the opposite direction to how it does in the other images.

Q5. D

The 'NO' sign has been replaced with an 'O' shape.

Q6. C

The rectangle and the pentagon have swapped places.

Q7. B

In Figure B, the arrow points the tip of the star rather than the corner of the arrow.

Q8. C

In Figure C, the direction of the arrows do not match those in the question figure.

Q9. B

The direction of the arrows in Figure B do not match the sample figure.

Q10. D

The sun and heart shapes are swapped

Q11. C

The diagonal lines in the top and bottom middle boxes are the wrong way round.

Q12. B

The black chevron on the outside is in the wrong place.

Q13. B

Two of the circles have swapped colour.

Q14. B

The white and grey dots inside the star have swapped places.

Q15. D

The two dashed lines have the wrong dash size and spacing.

Codes

Question 1. Which option is the correct code for figure 4? Tick your answer.

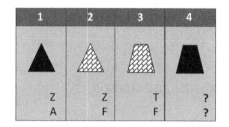
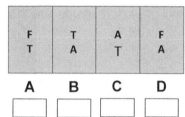

Question 2. Which option is the correct code for figure 4? Tick your answer.

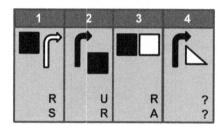
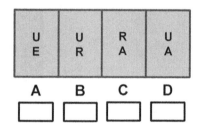

Question 3. Which option is the correct code for figure 4? Tick your answer.

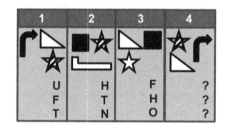
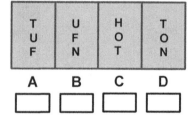

Question 4. Which option is the correct code for figure 4? Tick your answer.

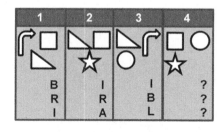
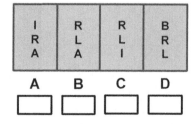

Question 5. Which option is the correct code for figure 4? Tick your answer.

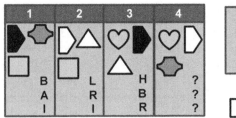
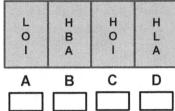

Question 6. Which option is the correct code for figure 4? Tick your answer.

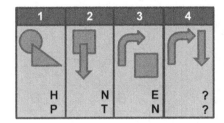
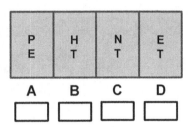

Question 7. Which option is the correct code for figure 4? Tick your answer.

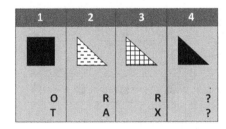
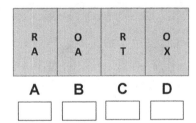

Question 8. Which option is the correct code for figure 4? Tick your answer.

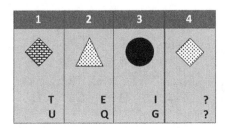
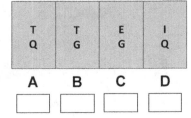

Question 9. Which option is the correct code for figure 4? Tick your answer.

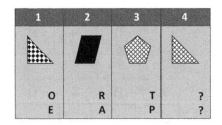

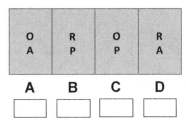

O	R	O	R
A	P	P	A
A	**B**	**C**	**D**

Question 10. Which option is the correct code for figure 4? Tick your answer.

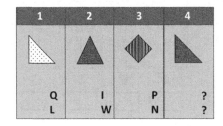

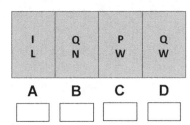

I	Q	P	Q
L	N	W	W
A	**B**	**C**	**D**

Question 11. Which option is the correct code for figure 4? Tick your answer.

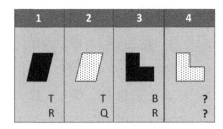

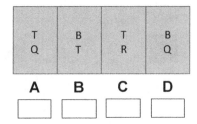

T	B	T	B
Q	T	R	Q
A	**B**	**C**	**D**

Question 12. Which option is the correct code for figure 4? Tick your answer.

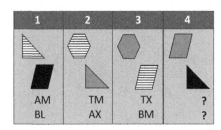

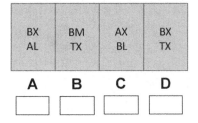

BX	BM	AX	BX
AL	TX	BL	TX
A	**B**	**C**	**D**

Question 13. Which option is the correct code for figure 4? Tick your answer.

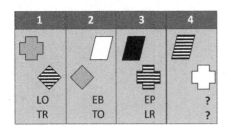 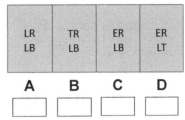

Question 14. Which option is the correct code for figure 4? Tick your answer.

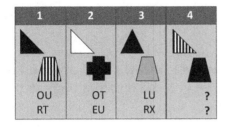 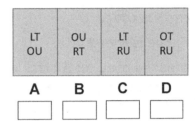

Question 15. Which option is the correct code for figure 4? Tick your answer.

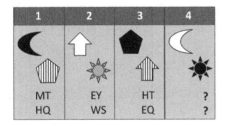 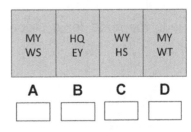

Answers to Codes

Q1. B = TA

The trapezium shape is coded 'T'

The triangle shape is coded 'Z'

The black colour is coded 'A'

The crossed pattern is coded 'F'

Figure 4 needs the code for a trapezium shape (T), filled with the colour black (A).

Q2. A = UE

The black square is coded 'R'.

The white arrow is coded 'S'.

The black arrow is coded 'U'.

The white square is coded 'A'.

Figure 4 needs the code for a black arrow (which is 'U'), and a white triangle. The white triangle did not appear, so the letter has to be different than all the previous letters.

Q3. A = TUF

The white triangle is coded 'F'.

The white star is coded 'O'.

The black square is coded 'H'.

Figure 4 needs the code for a striped star ('T'), a black arrow ('U') and a white triangle ('F').

Q4. B = RLA

The arrow is coded 'B'.

The square is coded 'R'.

The triangle is coded 'I'.

The circle is coded 'L'.

The star is coded 'A'.

Figure 4 needs the code for a square ('R'), a circle ('L') and a star ('A').

Q5. D = HLA

The black arrow shape is coded 'B'.

The grey cross shape is coded 'A'.

The grey square is coded 'I'.

The white 'arrow' shape is coded 'L'.

The grey heart is coded 'H'.

The white triangle is coded 'R'.

Figure 4 needs the codes for a grey heart (H), white arrow (L) and grey cross (A).

Q6. D = ET

The grey circle is coded 'H'.

The grey triangle is coded 'P'.

The grey arrow pointing to the right is coded 'E'.

The grey arrow pointing down is coded 'T'.

The grey square is coded 'N'.

Figure 4 needs the code for an arrow pointing to the right ('E') and an arrow pointing downwards ('T').

Q7. C = RT

The square is coded 'O'.

The right-angled triangle is coded 'R'.

The black pattern is coded 'T'.

The dotted lines are coded 'A'.

The square pattern is coded 'X'.

Figure 4 needs the code for a black right-angled triangle (which is 'R' and T).

Q8. A = TQ

The diamond is coded 'T'.

The triangle is coded 'E'.

The circle is coded 'I'.

The dotted pattern is coded 'Q'.

The brick pattern is coded 'U'.

The black pattern is coded 'G'.

Figure 4 needs the code for a diamond (T) with a dotted pattern (Q).

Q9. C = OP

The right-angled triangle is coded 'O'.

The parallelogram is coded 'R'.

The pentagon is coded 'T'.

The diagonal lines pattern is coded 'P'.

The checkered diamond pattern is coded 'E'.

The black pattern is coded 'A'.

Figure 4 needs the codes for a right-angled triangle (O) with diagonal lines (P).

Q10. D = QW

The right-angled triangle is coded 'Q'.

The equilateral triangle is coded 'I'.

The diamond is coded 'P'.

The checkered pattern is coded 'W'.

The dotted pattern is coded 'L'.

The vertical lines pattern is coded 'N'.

Figure 4 needs the codes for a right-angled triangle (Q) with a checkered pattern (W).

Q11. D = BQ

The L-Shape is coded 'B'.

The black colour is coded 'R'.

The parallelogram is coded 'T'.

The dotted pattern is coded 'Q'.

Figure 4 needs the code for L-Shape (B) and the dotted pattern (Q).

Q12. A = BX, AL

The parallelogram is coded 'B'.

The grey shade is coded 'X'.

The right-angled triangle is coded 'A'.

The black shade is coded 'L'.

The striped pattern is coded 'M'.

The hexagon is coded 'T'.

Figure 4 needs the code for parallelogram (B), grey shade (X), right-angled triangle (A), and black shade (L).

Q13. C = ER, LB

The parallelogram is coded 'E'.

The horizontal stripes pattern is coded 'R'.

The cross shape is coded 'L'.

The white shade is coded 'B'.

The diamond is coded 'T'.

Figure 4 needs the code for parallelogram (E), horizontal stripes (R), cross shape (L), and white shade (B).

Q14. D = OT, RU

The right-angled triangle is coded 'O'.

The white pattern is coded 'T'.

The trapezium shape is coded 'R'.

The black shade is coded 'U'.

The equilateral triangle is coded 'L'.

Figure 4 needs the code for right-angled triangle (O), vertical stripes (T), trapezium (R), and black shade (U).

Q15. D = MY, WT

The moon shape is coded 'M'.

The white shade is coded 'Y'.

The sun shape is coded 'W'.

The black pattern is coded 'T'.

The vertical stripes are coded 'Q'.

The grey shade is coded 'S'.

The arrow shape is coded 'E'.

Figure 4 needs the code for moon (M), white shade (Y), sun (W), and black shade (T).

Complete the Grid

Question 1. Which answer option completes the grid? Tick your answer.

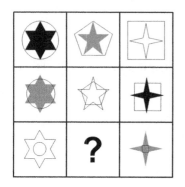 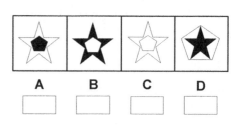

Question 2. Which answer option completes the grid? Tick your answer.

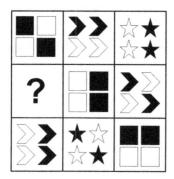 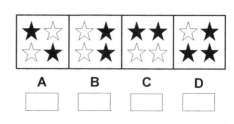

Question 3. Which answer option completes the grid? Tick your answer.

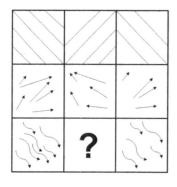 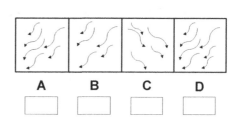

Question 4. Which answer option completes the grid? Tick your answer.

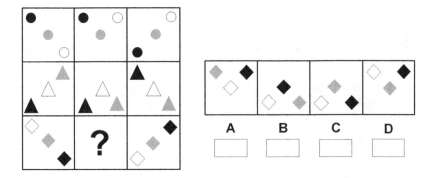

Question 5. Which answer option completes the grid? Tick your answer.

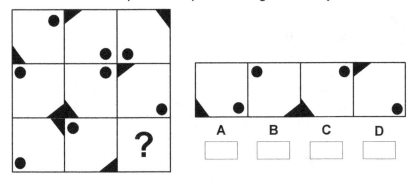

Question 6. Which answer option completes the grid? Tick your answer.

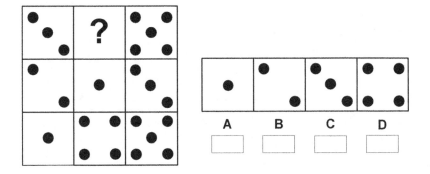

Question 7. Which answer option completes the grid? Tick your answer.

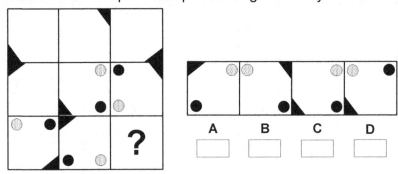

Question 8. Which answer option completes the grid? Tick your answer.

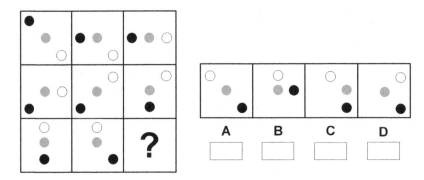

Question 9. Which answer option completes the grid? Tick your answer.

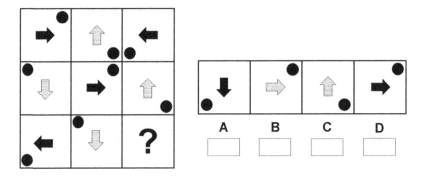

Question 10. Which answer option completes the grid? Tick your answer.

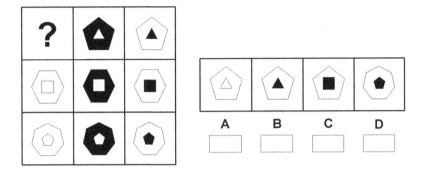

A B C D

Question 11. Which answer option completes the grid? Tick your answer.

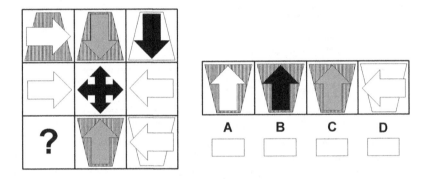

A B C D

Question 12. Which answer option completes the grid? Tick your answer.

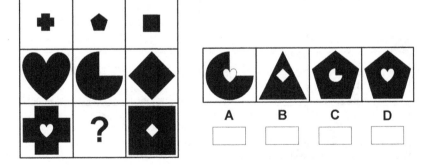

A B C D

Question 13. Which answer option completes the grid? Tick your answer.

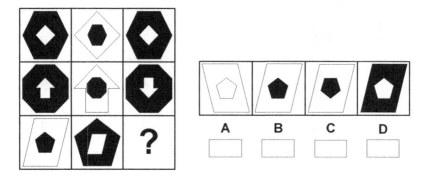

Question 14. Which answer option completes the grid? Tick your answer.

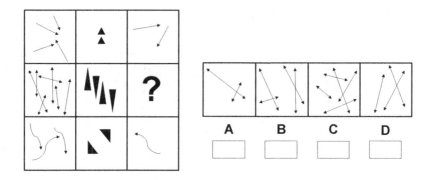

Question 15. Which answer option completes the grid? Tick your answer.

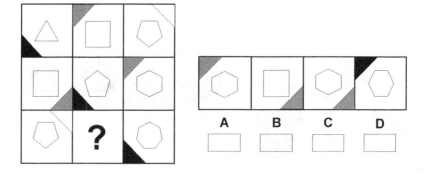

Answers to Complete the Grid

Q1. B

Column 1 contains a six-sided star and a circle.

Column 2 contains a five-sided star and a pentagon.

Column 3 contains a four sided star and a square.

The colour of the star alternates between black, grey, and white.

In each row the circle, pentagon, and square get smaller.

Q2. C

The sequence is as follows: four of the same shape in a 2 × 2 grid format.

The colour patterns change from being diagonal, top and bottom, and left and right.

In each row, the sequence moves the colour pattern along.

Q3. A

The number of lines in each row decreases by one

The number of lines in each column increases by one.

Q4. D

The sequence follows the colour pattern of: black, grey and white.

The shape in the bottom right corner moves to the top right corner to form the middle box in the row.

Then, the shape in the top left corner moves to the bottom left.

Q5. C

Both shapes stay diagonal to one another.

As the sequence progresses, the shapes move 90 degrees in a clockwise motion.

Q6. B

The first dots in the first two squares in each row are added together to equal the number of dots in the last square of each row.

Q7. C

In this sequence, the right-angled triangle moves to the opposite corner, then down to the lower corner. The circles maintain their position relative to the arrow.

Q8. A

In this sequence, the black and white circles take turns to move anti-clockwise around the grey central circle. This means that A is the correct answer option.

Q9. D

In this sequence, the central arrow rotates anti-clockwise, alternating between black and spotted. The circle orbits around the arrow in a clockwise direction.

Q10. A

The left column contains a white shape within another white shape.

Q11. B

The bottom-left space is a mirrored version of the top-right space, and the trapezium is striped.

Q12. C

The bottom square in each column is made up of the 2 shapes in the squares above it.

Q13. C

The left-hand column is identical to the right-hand column with the inside shape rotated 180°.

Q14. D

The number of triangles in the middle column determines how many less lines there will be in the right-hand column than the left-hand column.

Q15. C

Following the grid left to right, top to bottom, the triangle in the corner moves clockwise following the colour pattern, black, grey, white, grey then repeats.

The middle shapes follow the pattern of: increase by one edge, increase by one edge, decrease by one edge, then repeats, whilst rotating 90° anti-clockwise.

Like Shapes

For the following questions you need to identify the relationship between the top two figures and select the answer option that uses the same relationship for the bottom figure.

Question 1.

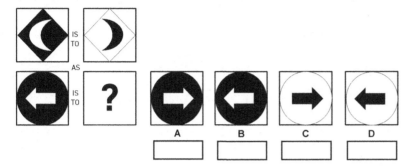

Question 2.

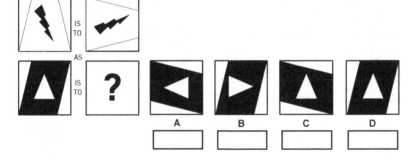

Question 3.

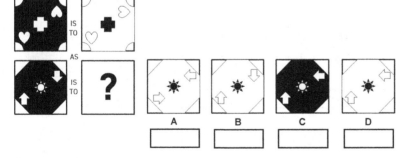

Question 4.

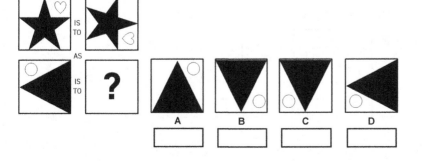

Question 5.

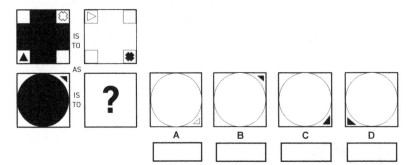

Question 6.

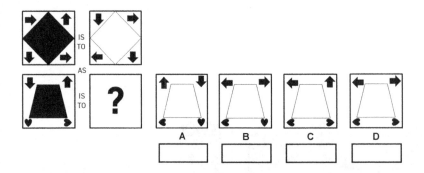

Question 7.

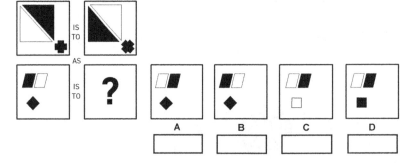

Question 8.

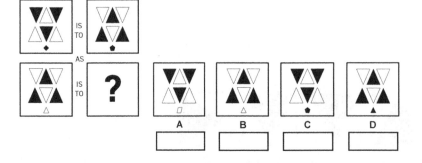

Question 9.

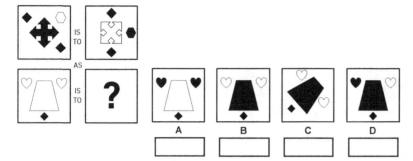

Question 10.

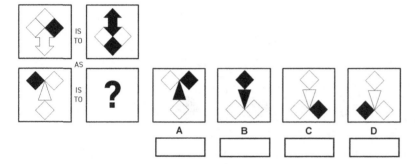

Question 11.

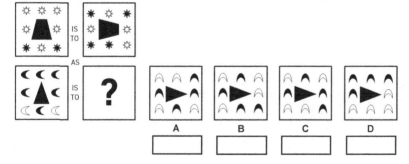

Question 12.

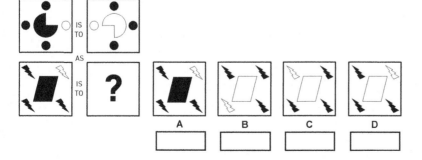

Question 13.

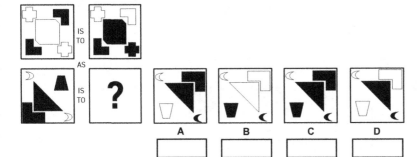

Question 14.

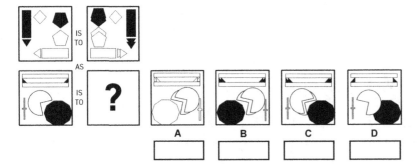

Question 15.

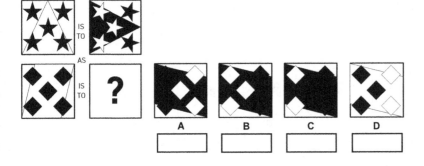

Answers to Like Shapes

Q1. C

The image is flipped horizontally, and the colours are inverted.

Q2. A

The large shape is rotated 90 degrees clockwise and the smaller inside shape is rotated 90 degrees anti-clockwise.

Q3. D

The colours of the box and the middle shape are inverted, and the top-right shape rotates 90 degrees clockwise.

Q4. A

The entire image rotates 90 degrees clockwise.

Q5. A

The images are rotated 90 degrees clockwise, and the colours are inverted.

Q6. B

The central image has its colours inverted. Then, the top two shapes rotate 90 degrees clockwise, the bottom left shape rotates 90 degrees clockwise, and the bottom right shape rotates 90 degrees clockwise.

Q7. D

The top two shapes switch colours, and the bottom shape rotates by 45 degrees.

Q8. A

The triangles invert their colours, and the bottom shape turns into another shape with an extra side.

Q9. C

The each shape rotates 45 degrees clockwise. Then, the central shape inverts its colour.

Q10. B

The shape flips vertically. Then, the central triangle shape turns to black, and the original black diamond shape turns back to white. The bottom diamond shape turns to black.

Q11. C

The entire image rotates 90 degrees clockwise. Then, the bottom middle and top right shapes invert colour.

Q12. B

The entire image rotates by 180 degrees. Then, the inside shape's colour is inverted.

Q13. B

The entire image rotates 180 degrees. The central shape and top right image invert colour. The bottom right shape inverts colour.

Q14. B

The entire image is mirrored and all shapes with an odd number of edges are doubled.

Q15. B

The entire image rotates 90 degrees clockwise. The back shape, and the two right-hand shapes, invert colour.

Cube Nets

Question 1. Which cube will the net make? Tick your answer.

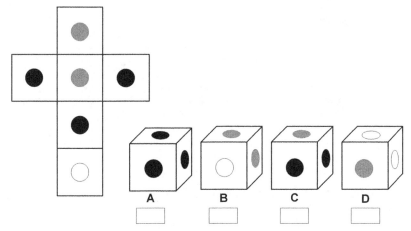

A   B   C   D

Question 2. Which cube will the net make? Tick your answer.

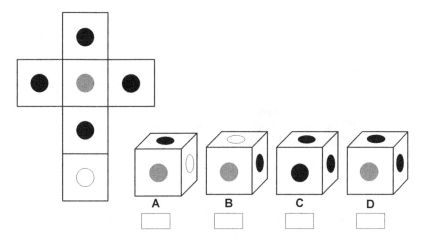

A   B   C   D

Question 3. Which cube will the net make? Tick your answer.

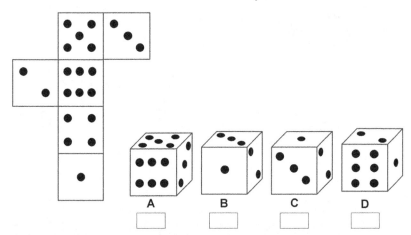

A   B   C   D

Question 4. Which cube will the net make? Tick your answer.

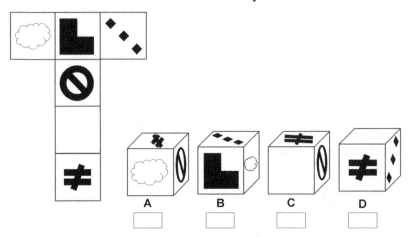

Question 5. Which cube will the net make? Tick your answer.

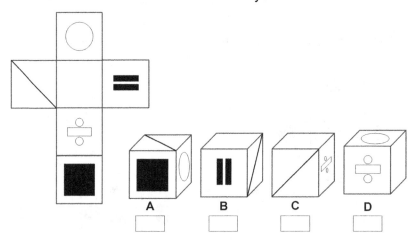

Question 6. Which cube will the net make? Tick your answer.

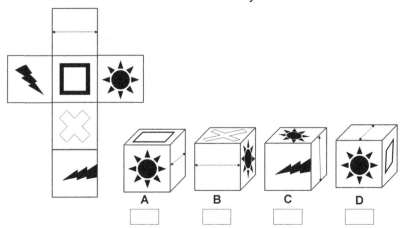

Question 7. Which cube will the net make? Tick your answer.

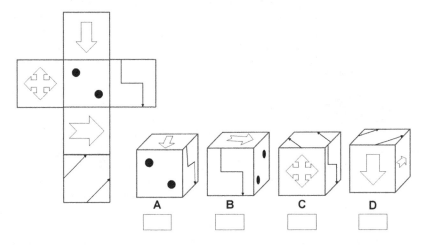

A   B   C   D

Question 8. Which cube will the net make? Tick your answer.

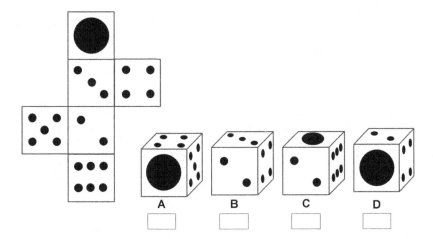

A   B   C   D

Question 9. Which cube will the net make? Tick your answer.

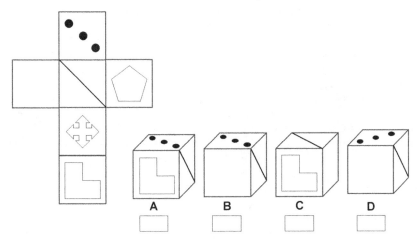

A   B   C   D

Question 10. Which cube **cannot** be made from the net? Tick your answer.

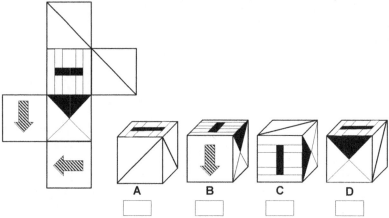

Question 11. Which cube **cannot** be made from the net? Tick your answer.

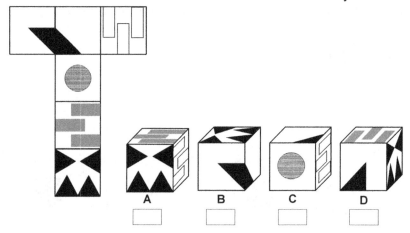

Question 12. Which cube **cannot** be made from the net? Tick your answer.

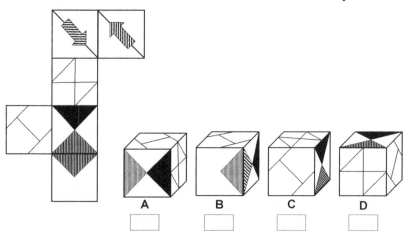

Question 13. Which cube **cannot** be made from the net? Tick your answer.

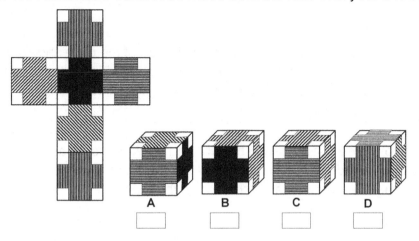

Question 14. Which cube **cannot** be made from the net? Tick your answer.

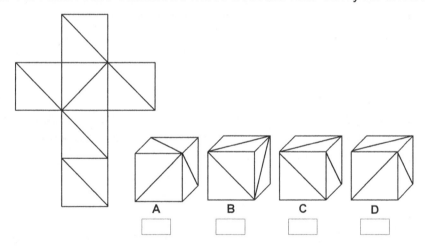

Question 15. Which cube will the net make? Tick your answer.

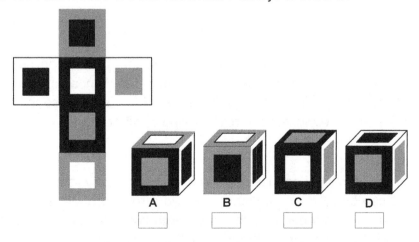

Answers to Cube Nets

Q1. C

Figure A can be ruled out, because the dot on the top of the cube should be grey, not black. Figure B can be ruled out, because the dot on top of the cube should be black. Figure D can be ruled out, because the dot on the side should be black, not white.

Q2. D

Figure A can be ruled out, because the dot on the side should be black, not white. Figure B can be ruled out, because the dot on the top should be black, not white. Figure C can be ruled out, because the dot on the top should be white, not black.

Q3. A

Figure B can be ruled out because the two dots would need to be replaced with the five dots. Figure C can be ruled out because the two dots would need to be replaced with the four dots. Figure D can be ruled out because the one dot would need to be replaced with the five dots.

Q4. D

Figure A can be ruled out because the 'no entry' sign cannot be on the right side of the 'cloud' shape. Figure B can be ruled out because the 'cloud' shape cannot be on the right side of the 'L' shape. Figure C can be ruled out because the 'no entry' sign would need to be replaced with the 'cloud' shape.

Q5. C

Figure A can be ruled out because the line on the top should be the 'equals' sign. Figure B can be ruled out because the side with the line on should have a circle instead. Figure D can be ruled out because there needs to be a space between the 'divide' sign and the circle.

Q6. A

Figure B can be ruled out because the arrow and the 'cross' sign need to be on opposite sides. Figure C can be ruled out because the 'sun' shape would need to be on the right side of the figure. Figure D can be ruled out because the two-pointed arrow, and the square would need to replace one another.

Q7. A

Figure B can be ruled out because the two dots are on the wrong side of the black line. Figure C can be ruled out because the two arrows are facing the wrong way. Figure D can be ruled out because the arrow with the cutaway and the other white arrow would not meet. Therefore, Figure A is the correct answer.

Q8. B

Figure A can be ruled out because the four dots would not appear next to the five dots. Figure C can be ruled out because the large dot would not be next to the two dots. This same rule can be applied to Figure D, leaving Figure B as the correct answer.

Q9. D

Figure B can be ruled out because the three dots are not in the right position. Figure C can be ruled out because the 'L' shape would not be next to the line or the blank space. This same rule applies to Figure A. Therefore, Figure D is the correct answer.

Q10. A

Figure A cannot be made, because the thick line along the top should be horizontal, not vertical.

Q11. C

Figure C cannot be made, because the triangle shape on the top of the cube, in the bottom right corner of the cube face, should be in the bottom left corner of the cube face.

Q12. D

Figure D cannot be made, because the pattern of the two triangles on the top of the cube need to switch. The top triangle should have a cross pattern, and the bottom triangle should be black.

Q13. A

Figure A cannot be made, because the diagonal lines on the top of the cube should go in the opposite direction.

Q14. D

Figure D cannot be made, because the diagonal line on the right face of the cube is going in the opposite direction.

Q15. A

Option B can be ruled out, because the black square inside the white square, on the side, should be a grey square inside a white square. Option C can be ruled out because the grey square inside the white square, on the side ,should be a black square inside of a white square. Option D can be ruled out because the black square inside a white square on the top, should be a white square inside a black square.

Spatial Reasoning

The definition of spatial reasoning is 'the ability to interpret and make drawings from mental images and visualise movement or change in those images.' The sample test questions within this guide will help you to improve in the areas of visualising and interpreting movement in shapes and diagrams.

It is important that, before you sit your test, you find out the type(s) of questions you will be required to answer. You should also take steps to find out if the tests will be timed and also whether or not they will be 'multiple-choice' based questions. If the tests that you will be required to undertake are timed and of multiple-choice in nature, then we strongly advise that you practise this type of test question.

Variety is the key to success. We recommend that you attempt a variety of different test questions, such as psychometric tests, numerical reasoning, verbal reasoning, fault analysis and mechanical reasoning etc. This will undoubtedly improve your overall ability to pass the test that you are required to undertake.

Confidence is an important part of test preparation. Have you ever sat a timed test and your mind goes blank? This is because your mind is focused on negative thoughts and your belief that you will fail the test. If you practise plenty of test questions under timed conditions then your confidence will grow. If your confidence is at its peak at the commencement of the test then there is no doubt that you will actually look forward to sitting the test, as opposed to being fearful of the outcome.

Aim for SPEED as well as ACCURACY. Many test centres want to see how quickly you can work, but they also want to see how accurate your work is, too. Therefore, when tackling the tests you must work as quickly as you can without sacrificing accuracy. Most tests are designed so that you do not finish them and you will most probably lose marks for incorrect answers.

2D views of 3D shapes.

Work out which figure is a top-down 2D view of the 3D question figure.

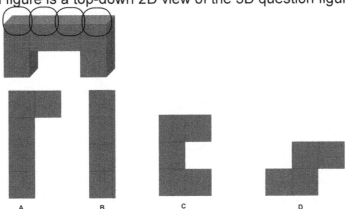

A   B   C   D

ANSWER = B

The key thing to remember about this type of question is positioning. If you do not look at the 3D object in the correct way, you will struggle to get the correct answer.

Take the sample question above, you will notice the circles highlighting the top of the 3D shape. Using this method, work out the 2D shape based on where the blocks are and how many you can see. For this question, you will notice that 4 squares would be seen if you were to look down on the object. The correct answer, is therefore B.

Building Blocks

Work out which 3D shapes from the answer options are needed to create the question figure.

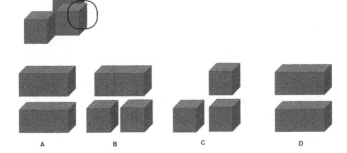

A   B   C   D

ANSWER = B

For these questions, blocks will be placed alongside, behind, on top of, or in front of one another; in order to make the question more challenging.

The circle is highlighting a taller cuboid behind the front cube. So, based on the answer options the only answer that would work would be answer B.

Hidden Shapes

Work out where the hidden shape is. The hidden shape can be found in one of the answer options. *It will be exactly the same size and same way round where it is hidden.*

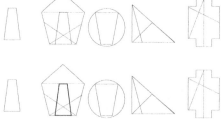

ANSWER = A

The importance of this question is to pay close attention to sizing and positioning. The shape may look the same, but it might not be. **Make sure the hidden shape is the exact same size and remember, it must remain the same way round where it is hidden.**

Connect the Shapes

Connect the shapes using the corresponding letters to match up the shapes.

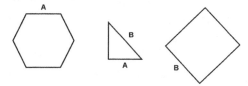

• Using the letters, match the sides of the shapes up with the corresponding letter.

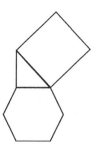

For spatial reasoning questions, your task is to look at the given shapes and decide which of the examples match the shape when joined together by the corresponding letters.

Pay close attention to the letters and the sides. The answer options may have been rotated. Therefore, you need to carefully work out which answer options best matches the Question Figures.

Connect the Shapes

Q1. Which answer option is made by joining all of the shapes together with the corresponding letters?

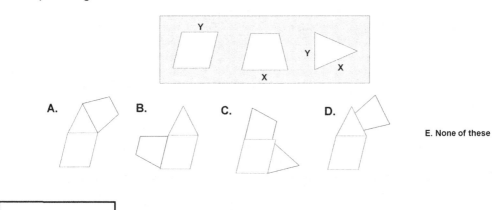

E. None of these

Q2. Which answer option is made by joining all of the shapes together with the corresponding letters?

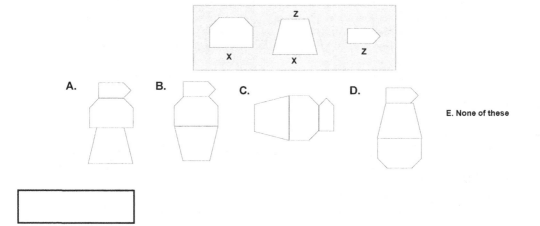

E. None of these

Q3. Which answer option is made by joining all of the shapes together with the corresponding letters?

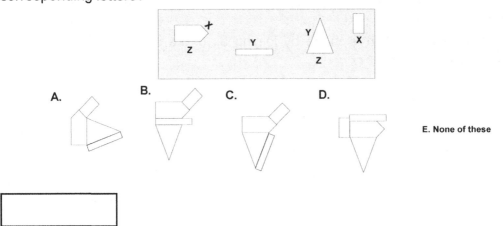

A. B. C. D.

E. None of these

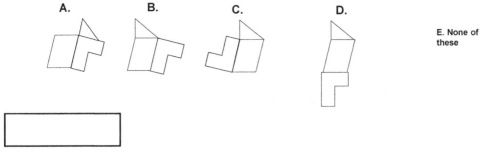

Q4. Which answer option is made by joining all of the shapes together with the corresponding letters?

A. B. C. D.

E. None of these

Q5. Which answer option is made by joining all of the shapes together with the corresponding letters?

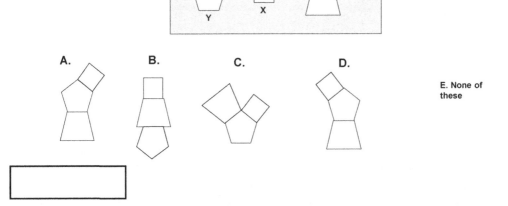

A. B. C. D.

E. None of these

Q6. Which answer option is made by joining all of the shapes together with the corresponding letters?

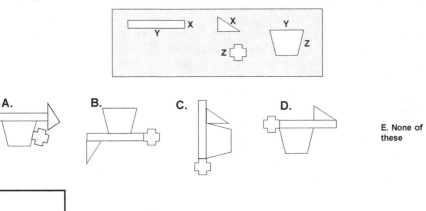

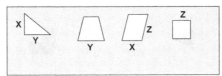

E. None of these

Q7. Which answer option is made by joining all of the shapes together with the corresponding letters?

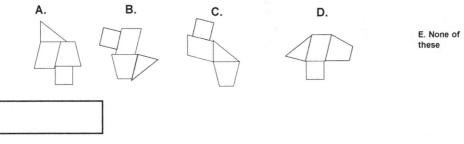

E. None of these

Q8. Which answer option is made by joining all of the shapes together with the corresponding letters?

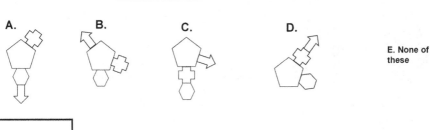

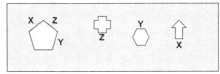

E. None of these

Q9. Which answer option is made by joining all of the shapes together with the corresponding letters?

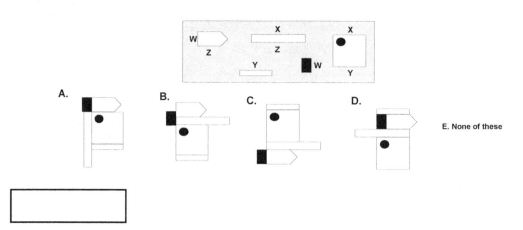

A.   B.   C.   D.   E. None of these

Q10. Which answer option is made by joining all of the shapes together with the corresponding letters?

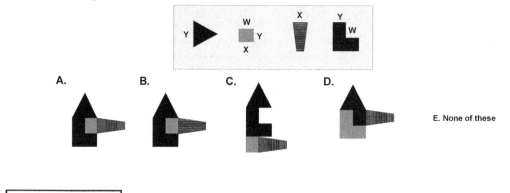

A.   B.   C.   D.   E. None of these

Q11. Which answer option is made by joining all of the shapes together with the corresponding letters?

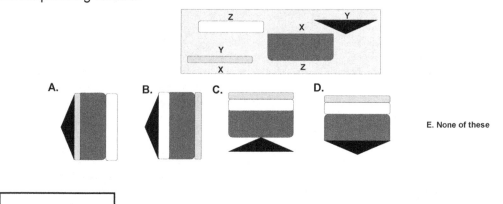

A.   B.   C.   D.   E. None of these

Q12. Which answer option is made by joining all of the shapes together with the corresponding letters?

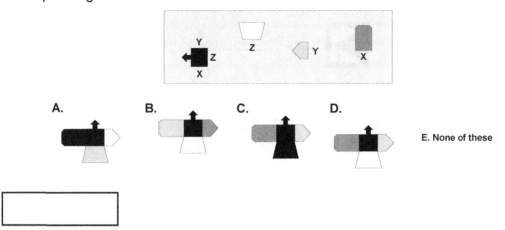

A.   B.   C.   D.   E. None of these

Q13. Which answer option is made by joining all of the shapes together with the corresponding letters?

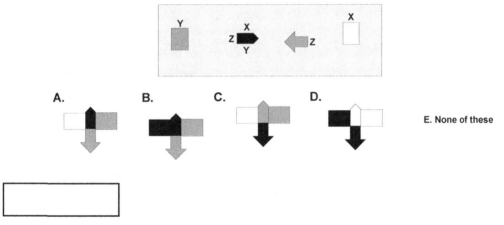

A.   B.   C.   D.   E. None of these

Q14. Which answer option is made by joining all of the shapes together with the corresponding letters?

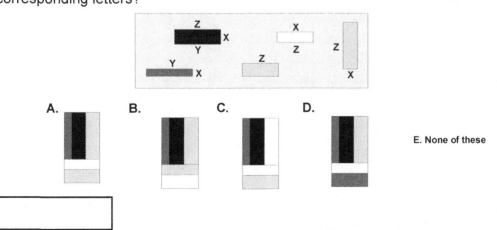

A.   B.   C.   D.   E. None of these

Q15. Which answer option is made by joining all of the shapes together with the corresponding letters?

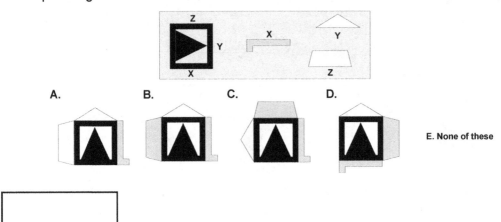

A.   B.   C.   D.

E. None of these

Answers to Connect the Shapes

Q1. A

Q2. D

Q3. C

Q4. B

Q5. D

Q6. A

Q7. C

Q8. E

Q9. E

Q10. A

Q11. A

Q12. D

Q13. A

Q14. E

Q15. A

Rotated Shapes

Question 1. Which answer option A, B, C, or D would look like the question figure if rotated exactly the same? Tick your answer.

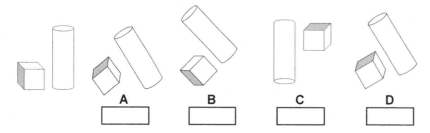

A	B	C	D

Question 2. Which answer option A, B, C, or D would look like the question figure if rotated exactly the same? Tick your answer.

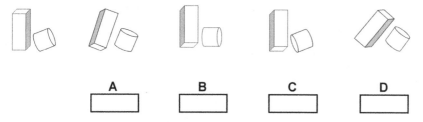

A	B	C	D

Question 3. Which answer option A, B, C, or D would look like the question figure if rotated exactly the same? Tick your answer.

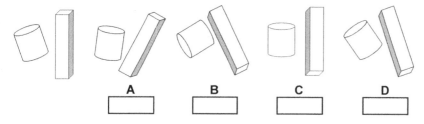

A	B	C	D

Question 4. Which answer option A, B, C, or D would look like the question figure if rotated exactly the same? Tick your answer.

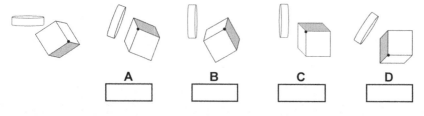

A	B	C	D

Question 5. Which answer option A, B, C, or D would look like the question figure if rotated exactly the same? Tick your answer.

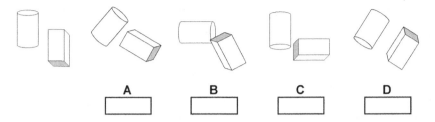

A	B	C	D

Question 6. Which answer option A, B, C, or D would look like the question figure if rotated exactly the same? Tick your answer.

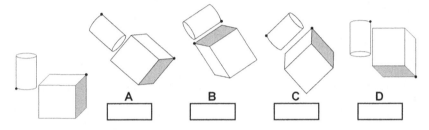

A	B	C	D

Question 7. Which answer option A, B, C, or D would look like the question figure if rotated exactly the same? Tick your answer.

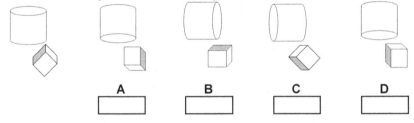

A	B	C	D

Question 8. Which answer option A, B, C, or D would look like the question figure if rotated exactly the same? Tick your answer.

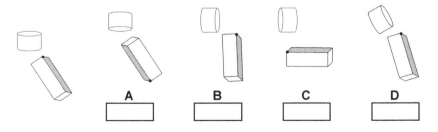

A	B	C	D

Question 9. Which answer option A, B, C, or D would look like the question figure if rotated exactly the same? Tick your answer.

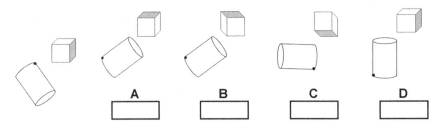

| A | B | C | D |

Question 10. Which answer option A, B, C, or D would look like the question figure if rotated exactly the same? Tick your answer.

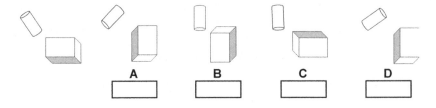

| A | B | C | D |

Question 11. Which answer option A, B, C, or D would look like the question figure if rotated exactly the same? Tick your answer.

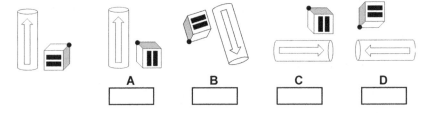

| A | B | C | D |

Question 12. Which answer option A, B, C, or D would look like the question figure if rotated exactly the same? Tick your answer.

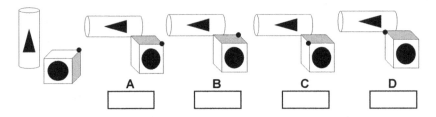

| A | B | C | D |

Question 13. Which answer option A, B, C, or D would look like the question figure if rotated exactly the same? Tick your answer.

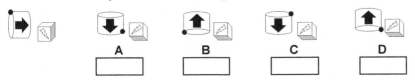

A	B	C	D

Question 14. Which answer option A, B, C, or D would look like the question figure if rotated exactly the same? Tick your answer.

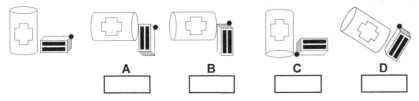

A	B	C	D

Question 15. Which answer option A, B, C, or D would look like the question figure if rotated exactly the same? Tick your answer.

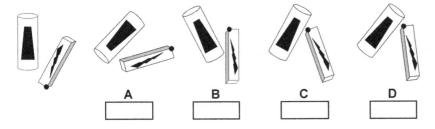

A	B	C	D

Answers to Rotated Shapes

Q1. B

Both shapes are rotated by 45 degrees anti-clockwise.

Q2. C

Both shapes are rotated by 180 degrees.

Q3. A

Both shapes are rotated 45 degrees clockwise

Q4. D

Both shapes are rotated by 135 degrees clockwise.

Q5. D

Both shapes are rotated 135 degrees anti-clockwise.

Q6. B

Both shapes are rotated 135 degrees clockwise.

Q7. C

Both shapes are rotated 90 degrees anti-clockwise.

Q8. A

Both shapes are rotated 180 degrees.

Q9. B

Both shapes are rotated 90 degrees anti-clockwise.

Q10. D

Both shapes are rotated 90 degrees clockwise.

Q11. B

Both shapes are rotated approximately 150 degrees clockwise.

Q12. D

Both shapes are rotated 90 degrees anti-clockwise. The dot is only in the correct position in option D.

Q13. C

Both shapes are rotated 90 degrees clockwise.

Q14. D

Both shapes are rotated 45 degrees anti-clockwise.

Q15. A

Both shapes are rotated 135 degrees anti-clockwise.

Hidden Shapes

Question 1. Which answer figure contains the hidden shape? The shape must be the same size and cannot be rotated. Tick your answer.

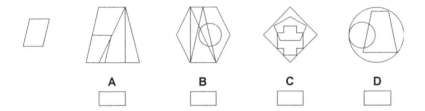

A	B	C	D
☐	☐	☐	☐

Question 2. Which answer figure contains the hidden shape? The shape must be the same size and cannot be rotated. Tick your answer.

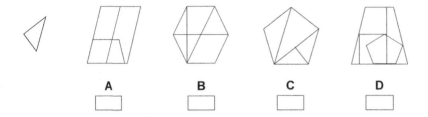

A	B	C	D
☐	☐	☐	☐

Question 3. Which answer figure contains the hidden shape? The shape must be the same size and cannot be rotated. Tick your answer.

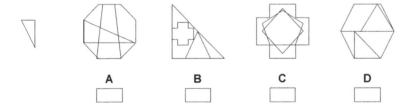

A	B	C	D
☐	☐	☐	☐

Question 4. Which answer figure contains the hidden shape? The shape must be the same size and cannot be rotated. Tick your answer.

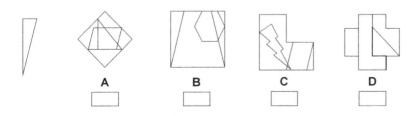

A	B	C	D
☐	☐	☐	☐

Question 5. Which answer figure contains the hidden shape? The shape must be the same size and cannot be rotated. Tick your answer.

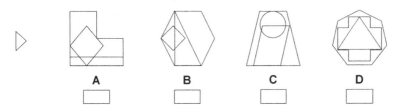

A	B	C	D

Question 6. Which answer figure contains the hidden shape? The shape must be the same size and cannot be rotated. Tick your answer.

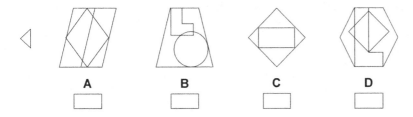

A	B	C	D

Question 7. Which answer figure contains the hidden shape? The shape must be the same size and cannot be rotated. Tick your answer.

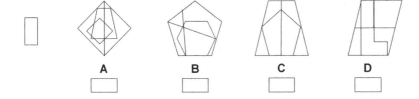

A	B	C	D

Question 8. Which answer figure contains the hidden shape? The shape must be the same size and cannot be rotated. Tick your answer.

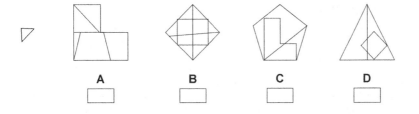

A	B	C	D

Question 9. Which answer figure contains the hidden shape? The shape must be the same size and cannot be rotated. Tick your answer.

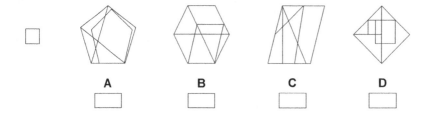

Question 10. Which answer figure contains the hidden shape? The shape must be the same size and cannot be rotated. Tick your answer.

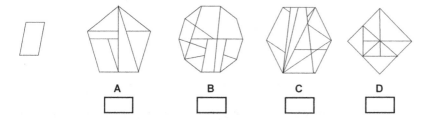

Question 11. Which answer figure contains the hidden shape? The shape must be the same size and cannot be rotated. Tick your answer.

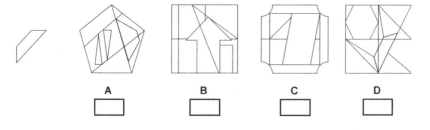

Question 12. Which answer figure contains the hidden shape? The shape must be the same size and cannot be rotated. Tick your answer.

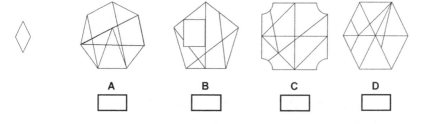

Question 13. Which answer figure contains the hidden shape? The shape must be the same size and cannot be rotated. Tick your answer.

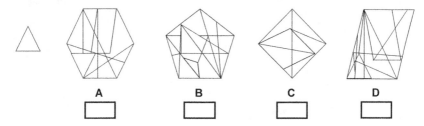

Question 14. Which answer figure contains the hidden shape? The shape must be the same size and cannot be rotated. Tick your answer.

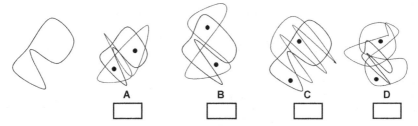

Question 15. Which answer figure contains the hidden shape? The shape must be the same size and cannot be rotated. Tick your answer.

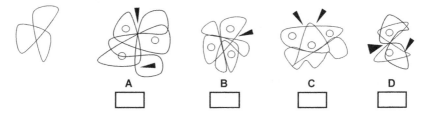

Answers to Hidden Shapes

Q1.C

Q2.A

Q3.D

Q4.B

Q5.B

Q6.C

Q7.D

Q8.B

Q9. D

Q10. B

Q11. D

Q12. D

Q13. D

Q14. C

Q15. B

2D Views of 3D Shapes

Question 1. Which answer option is a top-down 2D view of the question figure? Tick your answer.

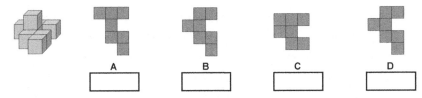

A   B   C   D

Question 2. Which answer option is a top-down 2D view of the question figure? Tick your answer.

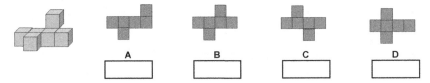

A   B   C   D

Question 3. Which answer option is a top-down 2D view of the question figure? Tick your answer.

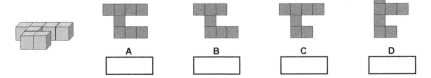

A   B   C   D

Question 4. Which answer option is a top-down 2D view of the question figure? Tick your answer.

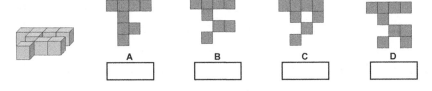

A   B   C   D

Question 5. Which answer option is a top-down 2D view of the question figure? Tick your answer.

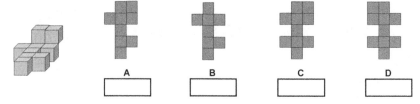

A
B
C
D

Question 6. Which answer option is a top-down 2D view of the question figure? Tick your answer.

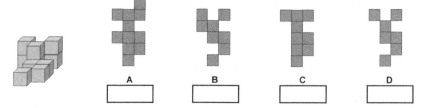

A
B
C
D

Question 7. Which answer option is a top-down 2D view of the question figure? Tick your answer.

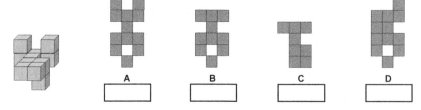

A
B
C
D

Question 8. Which answer option is a top-down 2D view of the question figure? Tick your answer.

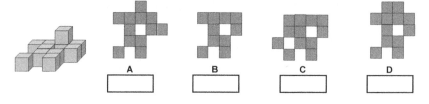

A
B
C
D

Question 9. Which answer option is a top-down 2D view of the question figure? Tick your answer.

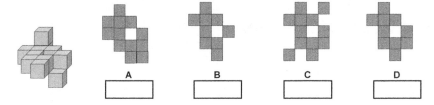

| A | B | C | D |

Question 10. Which answer option is a top-down 2D view of the question figure? Tick your answer.

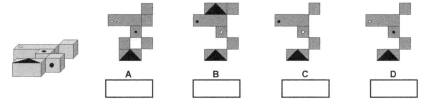

| A | B | C | D |

Question 11. Which answer option is a top-down 2D view of the question figure? Tick your answer.

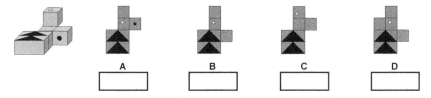

| A | B | C | D |

Question 12. Which answer option is a top-down 2D view of the question figure? Tick your answer.

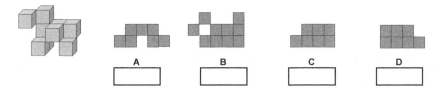

| A | B | C | D |

Question 13. Which answer option is a top-down 2D view of the question figure? Tick your answer.

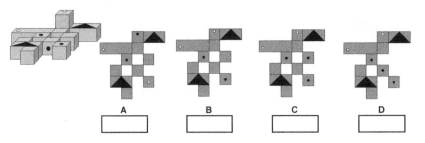

A ☐   B ☐   C ☐   D ☐

Question 14. Which answer option is a top-down 2D view of the question figure? Tick your answer.

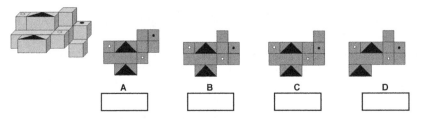

A ☐   B ☐   C ☐   D ☐

Question 15. Which answer option is a top-down 2D view of the question figure? Tick your answer.

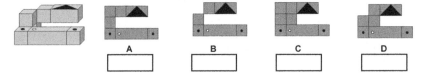

A ☐   B ☐   C ☐   D ☐

Answers to 2D Views of 3D Shapes

Q1. A

Q2. B

Q3. C

Q4. B

Q5. A

Q6. C

Q7. D

Q8. B

Q9. D

Q10. C

Q11. C

Q12. D

Q13. B

Q14. A

Q15. A

Figure Analysis

The pieces of paper below have been folded and then had holes punched in them.

Question 1. Which of the answer options would look like the unfolded paper? Tick your answer.

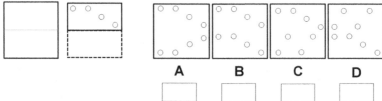

A   B   C   D

Question 2. Which of the answer options would look like the unfolded paper? Tick your answer.

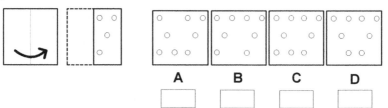

A   B   C   D

Question 3. Which of the answer options would look like the unfolded paper? Tick your answer.

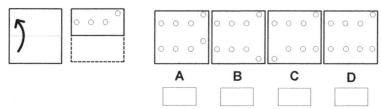

A   B   C   D

Question 4. Which of the answer options would look like the unfolded paper? Tick your answer.

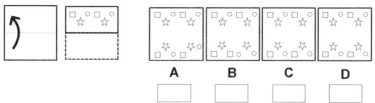

A   B   C   D

Question 5. Which of the answer options would look like the unfolded paper? Tick your answer.

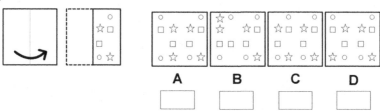

A   B   C   D

Question 6. Which of the answer options would look like the unfolded paper? Tick your answer.

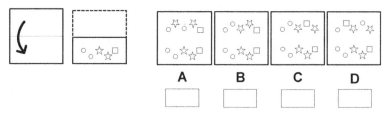

A	B	C	D

Question 7. Which of the answer options would look like the unfolded paper? Tick your answer.

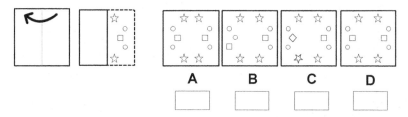

A	B	C	D

Question 8. Which of the answer options would look like the unfolded paper? Tick your answer.

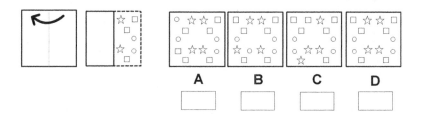

A	B	C	D

Question 9. Which of the answer options would look like the unfolded paper? Tick your answer.

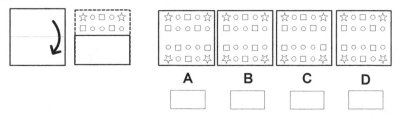

A	B	C	D

Question 10. Which of the answer options would look like the unfolded paper? Tick your answer.

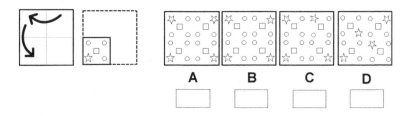

A	B	C	D

Question 11. Which of the answer options would look like the unfolded paper? Tick your answer.

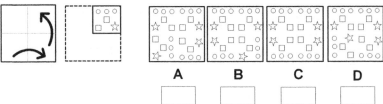

Question 12. Which of the answer options would look like the unfolded paper? Tick your answer.

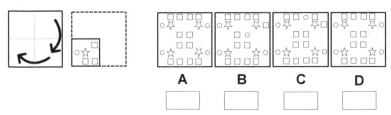

Question 13. Which of the answer options would look like the unfolded paper? Tick your answer.

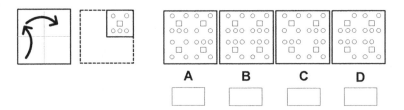

Question 14. Which of the answer options would look like the unfolded paper? Tick your answer.

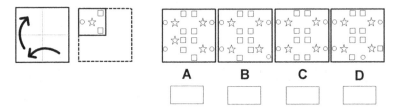

Question 15. Which of the answer options would look like the unfolded paper? Tick your answer.

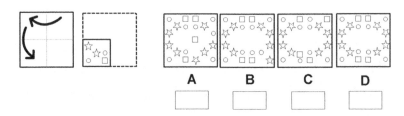

Answers to Figure Analysis

Q1. A

Q2. D

Q3. B

Q4. C

Q5. D

Q6. B

Q7. D

Q8. D

Q9. B

Q10. A

Q11. C

Q12. D

Q13. B

Q14. C

Q15. D

Blocks

Question 1. Which of the answer options contains the correct blocks to create the question figure? Tick your answer.

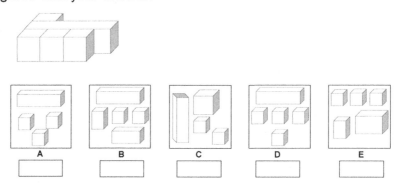

Question 2. Which of the answer options contains the correct blocks to create the question figure? Tick your answer.

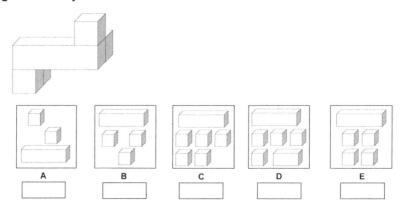

Question 3. Which of the answer options contains the correct blocks to create the question figure? Tick your answer.

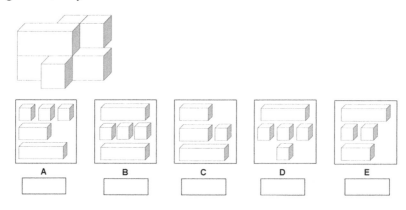

Question 4. Which of the answer options contains the correct blocks to create the question figure? Tick your answer.

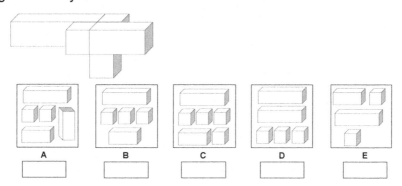

Question 5. Which of the answer options contains the correct blocks to create the question figure? Tick your answer.

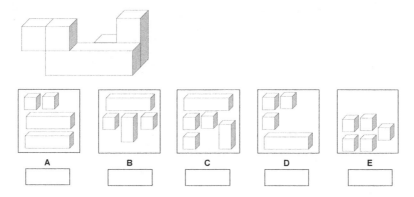

Question 6. Which of the answer options contains the correct blocks to create the question figure? Tick your answer.

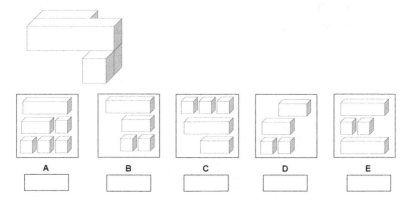

Question 7. Which of the answer options contains the correct blocks to create the question figure? Tick your answer.

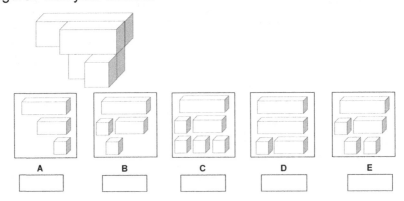

Question 8. Which of the answer options contains the correct blocks to create the question figure? Tick your answer.

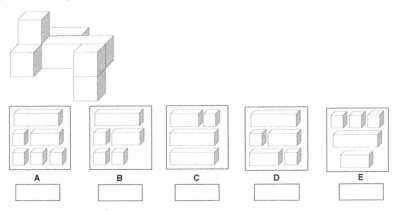

Question 9. Which of the answer options contains the correct blocks to create the question figure? Tick your answer.

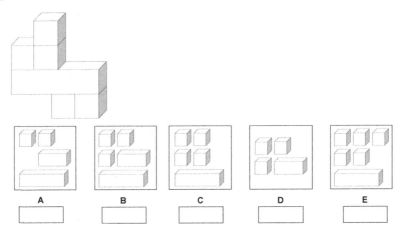

Question 10. Which of the answer options contains the correct blocks to create the question figure? Tick your answer.

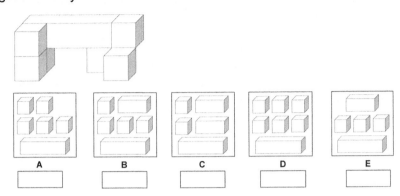

A	B	C	D	E

Question 11. Which of the answer options contains the correct blocks to create the question figure? Tick your answer.

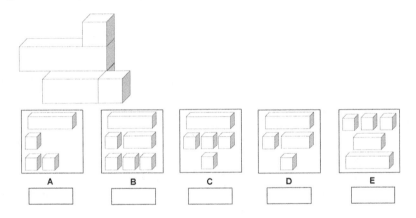

A	B	C	D	E

Question 12. Which of the answer options contains the correct blocks to create the question figure? Tick your answer.

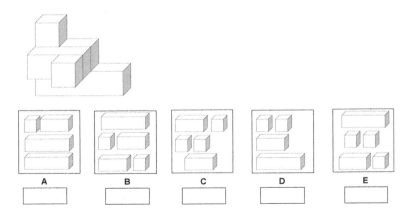

A	B	C	D	E

Question 13. Which of the answer options contains the correct blocks to create the question figure?

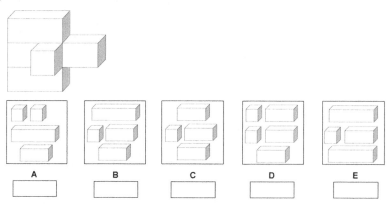

Question 14. Which of the answer options contains the correct blocks to create the question figure?

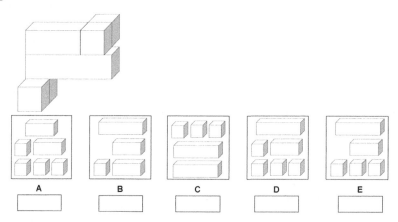

Question 15. Which of the answer options contains the correct blocks to create the question figure?

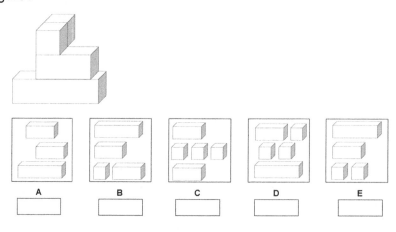

Answers to Blocks

Q1. D

Q2. E

Q3. A

Q4. B

Q5. C

Q6. B

Q7. E

Q8. A

Q9. E

Q10. D

Q11. E

Q12. B

Q13. B

Q14. D

Q15. E

Mechanical Aptitude

As part of the selection process for the job you're applying to, you may be required to sit a Mechanical Comprehension (or Mechanical Reasoning) test. Mechanical Comprehension tests your ability to understand mechanical concepts such as force, gravity, weight, mass, momentum, electronics, and more.

Mechanical Comprehension is a combination of practical knowledge of mechanical objects and how forces interact with them, as well as the ability to apply mathematical formulae to real-life situations.

For example, you may be asked to calculate the mechanical advantage of a pulley system, or the acceleration of an object. Likewise, you may be asked to pick the right tool for a specific job, such as stripping insulation from wires.

Essentially, Mechanical Comprehension tests a wide range of different ideas and concepts. We believe that the best way to prepare for these questions is to learn the rules and explanations for the different mechanical concepts, and then apply your knowledge using practice questions. Here, we'll be taking a look at explanations for the following key areas:

- Mechanical advantage and pulleys;

- Cogs, clockwise, and anti-clockwise;

- Forces (such as friction and gravity);

- Balancing weights;

- Circuits;

- PSI;

- Speed, distance, and time.

Mechanical Advantage and Pulleys

You may find that some mechanical comprehension tests ask you to calculate the mechanical advantage of a simple pulley system.

With fixed pulleys, the way to ascertain the force required to support the weight is dependent on two variables, the supporting ropes and the conversion between kg and newton 1kg = 9.8 newton.

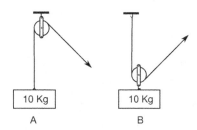

Diagram A = there is only one section of rope supporting the weight, therefore this can be worked out by just converting kg to newton 10 × 9.8 = 98 N.

Diagram B = there are two ropes supporting the weight, therefore this can be worked out by: 10 (weight) ÷ 2 (number of ropes supporting the weight) = 5, then 5 × 9.8 = 49 N.

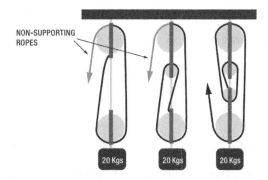

If you study the three pulley systems above, you will note that each system has both supporting ropes and non-supporting ropes. Supporting ropes are ones which, as the name suggests, support the load. Only the first two pulley systems have non-supporting ropes which we have indicated.

The non-supporting ropes in the first two pulley systems above simply change the direction of the force.

To calculate the mechanical advantage in a moveable pulley system, we simply have to count the number of supporting ropes. Counting the supporting ropes in the pulley systems above, the mechanical advantage of each of system is, from left to right 2, 3, and 5.

Gears, Clockwise, and Anti-Clockwise

If gears are connected by a chain or belt, then the gears will all move in the same direction.

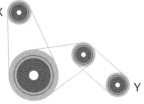

Questions involving cogs take two main forms. The first will require you to figure out whether a cog (or multiple cogs) is rotating clockwise or anti-clockwise. The simple rule here is that cogs connected in a series will alternate a rotation.

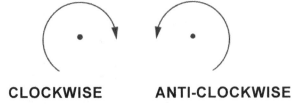

If the gears are touching, then adjacent gears move in the opposite direction. In the example above, X and Y will move in opposite directions.

CLOCKWISE   **ANTI-CLOCKWISE**

The easiest way to remember the above is to think of the way that the hands on a clock rotate; hence the phrase 'clockwise'.

You may also find that some test questions which have been created in the USA refer to anti-clockwise as 'counter-clockwise'.

The other type of cog question will require you to calculate the revolutions per minute (or rpm) of 2 or more cogs. The rpm of two cogs will depend on the size of the cog, which is usually determined by how many "teeth" it has. Working out rpm is usually straightforward:

Cog A is moving at 10 rpm, with 10 teeth, clockwise.

Cog B is twice the size of Cog A. This means that it will do half as many revolutions per minute as Cog A. So, 10 / 2 = 5 rpm.

Let's say that Cog B is 50% larger than Cog A, and has 15 teeth. Cog B is 1.5 times bigger than Cog A. Therefore, 10 / 1.5 = 6.66. Therefore, the rpm of Cog B is 6.66.

As a general rule, the smaller cog makes more revolutions per minute, as it has to turn more to match the turns of the larger cog.

Springs

When springs are arranged in a series, each spring can be the subject of the force applied. If the springs are arranged in a parallel line, the force is divided equally between them.

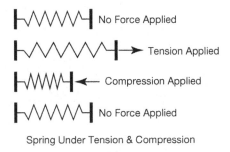

Spring Under Tension & Compression

Gravity

Force is measured in newtons (N). Earth has a gravitational field strength of 9.8 N/kg. So, 1 kg of mass = 9.8 N. So, if something has a mass of 50 kg it weighs 490 kg (50 kg × 9.8 N).

So, Weight = Mass × Gravitational Field Strength. On Earth the gravitational field strength is always 9.8 N. In contrast, the gravitational field strength on the moon is 1.6 N/kg.

'Work done' is another equation related to gravity. Work is done when a force causes objects to move. So, if you push a crate, work is done. The equation for this is:

Work Done = Force × Distance

Work Done is measured in joules (J) or newton-metres (Nm). 1 joule = 1 newton-metre.

For example, a crate weighs 500 N (force) and is pushed 50 m. The work done by the lift is:

500 N × 50 m = 25,000 J = 25 kJ (kilojoules).

Circuits

Questions regarding circuits usually follow a similar format, which will include: a power source, switches, bulbs and a path of wiring.

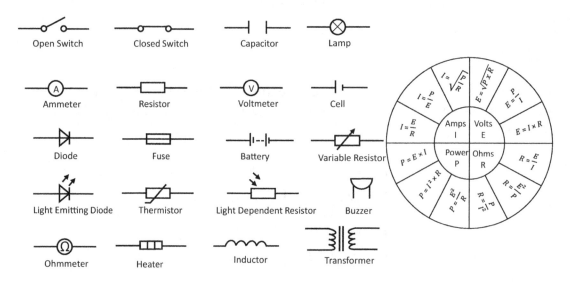

Voltage

Voltage is also known as the potential difference or electromotive force (e.m.f.). The potential difference is needed to make an electrical current flow through an electrical component. For example, cells and batteries are often used to provide the potential difference needed in a circuit.

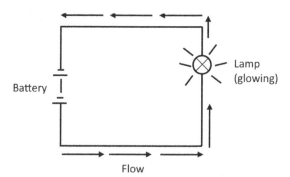

In the above electrical circuit, you will notice that there is only one source of potential difference (the battery). There is also only one source of resistance (the lamp).

Ohm's Law

Ohm's law is often used to analyse the electrical components within a circuit. In simple terms, Ohm's law specifically focuses on three electrical concepts:

- Potential difference (voltage);

- Current;

- Resistance.

The resistance of an electrical outlet can be found by measuring the current flow and the potential difference, i.e. the voltage running through it.

There is a simple equation to use in order to work out the relationship between current, resistance and potential difference.

REMEMBER the following equation:

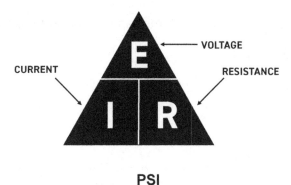

PSI

PSI is a measurement for pressure, and is measured by dividing the force of an object in pounds (lbs) by the area it's in (in square inches).

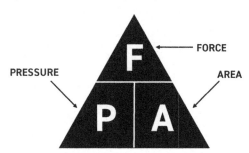

For example, if the force of the object is 50 lbs and the area is 2 square inches, then the PSI is 25:

50 / 2 = 25.

Speed, Distance, and Time

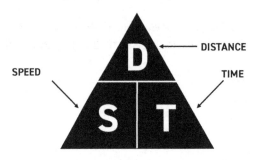

There are three equations that you need to know:

Distance = Speed × Time

For example, 60 mph × 10 hours = 600 miles.

Speed = Distance / Time

For example, 100 m / 10 seconds = 10 metres per second (10 m/s)

Time = Distance / Speed

For example, 60 miles / 30 mph = 2 hours.

Levers and Forces

A lever consists of a bar which is balanced on a fixed point, known as the fulcrum.

If you needed to lift the weight, you will need to calculate the weight placed at the opposite end.

Formula:

Weight required = (weight × distance from fulcrum to weight) ÷ distance from fulcrum point where weight is being applied.

- F = (10 × 3) / 3.

- F = 30 / 3

- F = 10 kg

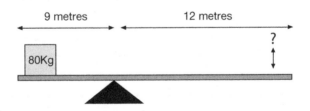

- F = (80 × 9) / 12

- F = 720 / 12

- F = 60 kg

Striking Tools

Sledge	A sledgehammer is a large, flat, often metal head, attached to a handle. It is used to break rock.
Hammer	A hammer is a tool with a heavy metal head used for driving in nails and breaking things.
Mallet	A mallet can be made from metal, plastic, wood, rubber or rawhide. This is used to strike another tool or surface without damaging it.

Fastening Tools

Allen Wrench	A tool to drive bolts and screws with hexagonal sockets in their heads.
Box Wrench	A wrench with a closed socket that covers over a nut or bolt head.
Cutting Pliers	A tool used to cut material such as wire.
Curved-Nose Pliers	A tool used to cut and hold material. Used to bend, re-position, or snip.
Long-Nosed Pliers	A tool used to cut and hold material. Used to bend, re-position, or snip.
Offset Screwdriver	A screwdriver with a blade at a right angle to the shaft.
Open-End Wrench	A wrench with jaws having a fixed width of opening at one or both ends.
Phillips Screwdriver	A screwdriver that has a cross-shaped tip.
Pipe Wrench	A tool used for turning soft pipes and fittings with a rounded surface.
Pliers	Pincers used for gripping or bending wire.
Slip-Joint Pliers	Pliers with a pivot point that can be altered to increase the size range of the jaws.
Socket Wrench	A ratchet tool with a series of detachable sockets for tightening and loosening nuts.
Standard Screwdriver	A tool used for turning a screw. This type of screwdriver will have a long, flat head.
Stapler	A device used for fastening objects together with the use of staples.
Torque Wrench	A tool used for setting and adjusting the tightness of nuts and bolts.
Wrench	A tool used to turn something.
Wrench Pliers	A tool with derrated jaws that clamp objects.

Cutting Tools

Bolt Cutters	When the handles are closed, the shears are able to slice through metal objects.
Circle Snips	Circle snips are used to cut curves.
Coping Saw	Coping saws are a type of handsaw that is used to cut shapes or curved lines.
Crosscut Saw	Crosscut saws are a type of handsaw that cuts against the grain of wood.
Hacksaw	A hacksaw is used to cut metal.
Pipe Cutters / Tube Cutters	This is a type of cutter that is used to score and cut metal objects.
Ripsaw	A ripsaw is a type of handsaw that cuts against the grain of wood.
Snips and Shears	Snips and shears have cutting blades (like scissors) which can be used to cut curved or straight.

Chisels

Metal-Cutting Chisels	Chisels that are able to cut into metal. Usually struck with a mallet.
Wood-Cutting Chisels	Chisels that are able to cut into wood. Socket chisels are struck with a mallet to cut through wood. Other chisels require only pressure from your hands.

Drills

Auger Bits	Auger bits pierce large holes.
Countersink	A countersink is a drill which enlarges the surface of a hole so a screw can be inserted.
Twist Drills	Twist drills are used to create holes.

Clamping Tools

Bench Vise	A vise with large jaws which holds material in place.
Clamps	Used when a vise doesn't work. Clamps generally connect to the items (not on a bench)
Handscrew Vise	A vise with two jaws connected by screws. The screws are used to tighten the vise together.
Pipe Vise	A vise that holds round pipes or trims.
Pliers	Pliers can be used to hold objects.
Vises	Hold material while being sawed, drilled or glued.

Finishing Tools

Double-Cut	Double cut files are used for rough work.
Flat Files and Half-Round	Files that are used for general purposes.
Single-Cut	Files that are used for finishing work and sharpening blades.
Square and Round	Files fit square and/or round openings.

Measuring Tools

Calipers	Calipers are used for very small and exact measurements.
Depth Gauges	Depth gauges measure the depths of holes.
Tape Rules	Tape rules are used to measure material.
Level	Levels are a tool which allow you to see if the surface is level.
Square Level	A square level is used to check the accuracy of an angle.
Thickness Gauges	Thickness gauges measure the thickness of holes.
Wire Gauges	Wire gauges measure the thickness of wire.

Fastening Bits

Bolts	Bolts are flat ended and are held in place by a nut and washer.
Brads and Finishing Nails	These type of nails have heads which are made to fit in line or slighly below the surface of wood.
Common Nails	These are nails that are used for general purposes.
Double-Headed Nails	This type of nail has two heads, one lower than the other. The nail is driven into an object until it reaches the lower head, but can be pulled out by the higher head.
Lag Screws	Lag screws have square or hexagonal shaped heads.
Machine Screws	Machine screws are used for metal. They come in various sizes and have a variety of different heads.
Nuts	Nuts can come in different shapes. They can be square or hexagonal. Cap nuts are round and smooth. Stop nuts prevent screws or bolts from coming loose. Wing nuts have 'wings' on each side so they can be tightened by hand.
Rivets	Rivets are used to fasten metal objects together.
Washers	Washers prevent damage to a surface by preventing the bolt from digging into the materia.
Wood Screws	Wood screws are used to fasten wood objects together.

Mechanical Comprehension Test 1

Question 1. If the object has the same density throughout, which cable is carrying the least weight? If equal, select C for your answer.

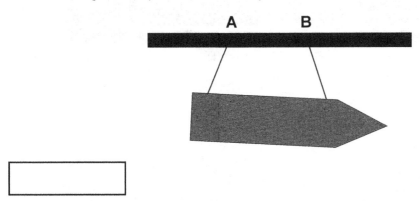

Question 2. Which box is the heaviest?

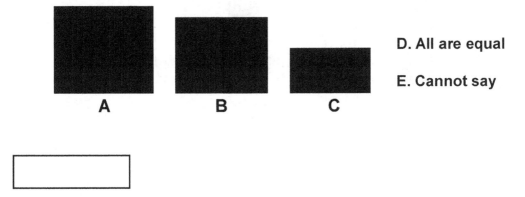

D. All are equal

E. Cannot say

A   B   C

Question 3. If a weight was placed on top of the pile of bricks below, which pile could take the heaviest weight? Circle your answer.

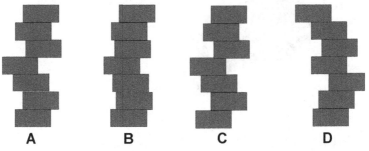

A   B   C   D

Question 4. If both trucks were involved in a head on collision with another vehicle whilst travelling at the same velocity, which one would cause the least damage? If the damage would be equal, select C for your answer.

A   B

Question 5. Which pulley system is the least effective at lifting the 10 kg weight?

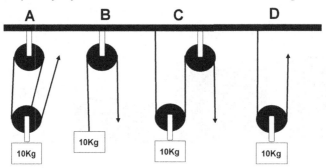

Question 6. In which direction does friction act on the truck?

Question 7. If cog B turns anti-clockwise, which way will cog A turn? Select C if the cog won't move.

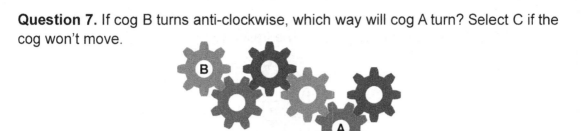

```
┌──────────────────┐
│                  │
│                  │
└──────────────────┘
```

Question 8. How much weight needs to be placed at point X to balance the beam?

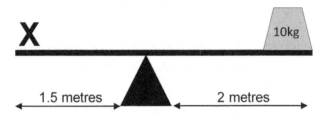

```
┌──────────────────┐
│                  │
│                  │
└──────────────────┘
```

Question 9. If cog A turns clock-wise, how many cogs will turn anti-clockwise?

```
┌──────────────────┐
│                  │
│                  │
└──────────────────┘
```

Question 10. If the driver of the following right-hand drive car reverses whilst turning the wheel to the left, which direction will the trailer go?

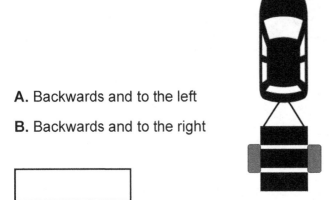

A. Backwards and to the left

B. Backwards and to the right

Question 11. If the following cog and belt system rotates at 1200rpm for ten minutes, which cog will rotate the greatest number of times? Select C if you believe the cogs will rotate an equal number.

A
B

Question 12. In which direction will the canoe travel if the canoeist loses his left paddle but continues to use the right one only?

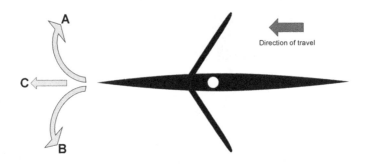

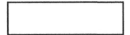

Question 13. How much weight should be placed at point X to balance the beam?

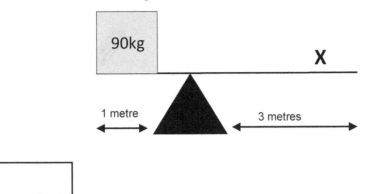

```
┌─────────────┐
```

Question 14. If the following vinyl record spins at 45 rpm for 2 minutes, which point will make the greatest number of revolutions? If you believe they will all revolve an equal number, select D as your answer.

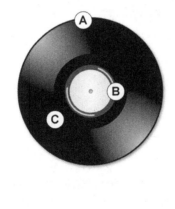

```
┌─────────────┐
```

Question 15. Which of the following tools is best for removing nails from wood?

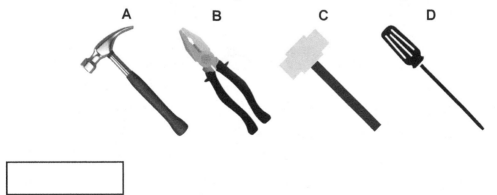

```
┌─────────────┐
```

Question 16. Which of the following tools is best for stripping away insulation from electrical wires?

A   B   C   D

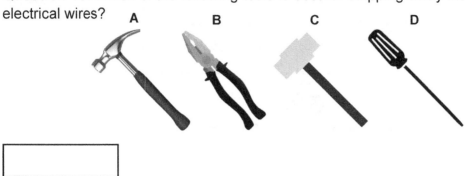

```
┌─────────────────┐
│                 │
│                 │
└─────────────────┘
```

Question 17. Which way would you turn the bolt in order to tighten it?

A   B

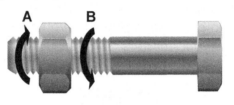

```
┌─────────────────┐
│                 │
│                 │
└─────────────────┘
```

Question 18. Which load will be the easiest to lift?

X   Y   Z

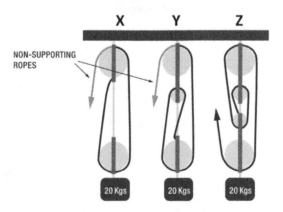

```
┌─────────────────┐
│                 │
│                 │
└─────────────────┘
```

Question 19. If water flows through the pipe from point A to B, at which point will the velocity be the greatest?

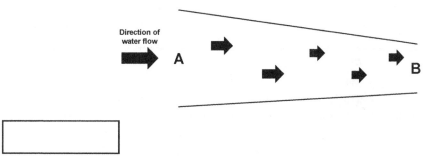

Question 20. A glass beaker contains oil and water as depicted below. If more water is poured into the beaker, how will it look (A, B or C)?

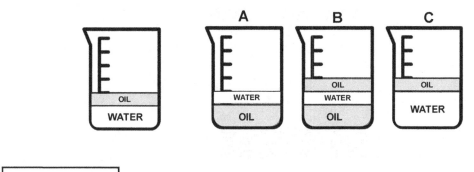

Question 21. In which direction is the truck moving? If the truck is stationary, select C for your answer.

Question 22. How much weight is required at point X to balance the load?

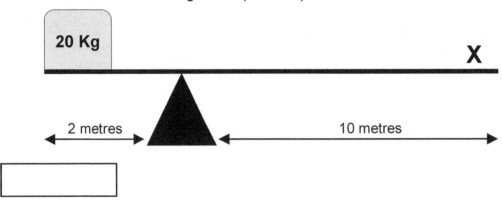

Question 23. How much force is required to lift the following 60 kg load?

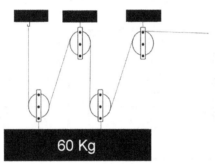

Question 24. Why are convex mirrors commonly used on vehicles? Circle your answer.

A. The reflection of images are clearer.

B. Convex mirrors don't distort moving images.

C. Vibrations from movement are countered when using a convex mirror.

D. They provide a wider field-of-view.

Question 25. If a force of 60 pounds is exerted over an area of 2 square foot, what is the psi?

Answers to Mechanical Comprehension Test 1

Q1. A

B is carrying more weight as the object is tilted downwards.

Q2. E

Although the boxes are all different sizes, we are unable to say which is heaviest. On that basis, the only viable answer is E, cannot say.

Q3. B

The bricks in pile B are stacked more neatly and narrowly than the rest. Therefore, the force applied by the weight is less likely to cause the pile to collapse.

Q4. A

Truck A would cause the least damage due to the fact it is carrying the least amount of weight. If the trucks are travelling at the same velocity upon impact, truck B will have a greater impact due to the additional weight being carried.

Q5. B

Pulley System B has no supporting ropes, and therefore has no mechanical advantage. Therefore, it is the least effective system for lifting the 10 kg weight.

Q6. A

Friction acts between the tires and the ground, working against the direction of the vehicle. Therefore, while the truck might be moving downhill, friction is working against it up the hill.

Q7. Anti-clockwise

The cogs that are connected will alternate in direction.

Q8. 7.5 kg

$10 \div 2 = 2.5$

$10 \div 2.5 = 7.5$ kg

Q9. 1

Only the first three cogs are interconnected. This means only one of them will rotate anti-clockwise.

Q10. B

Trailers are hitched to cars using ball-and-socket connections. This acts as a pivot. So, when the car reverses and turns the wheel to the left, the rear of the car will start to turn towards the left. Since the connection is a pivot, this causes the trailer to move backwards, and to the right.

Q11. B

Because wheel B is smaller, it will rotate the most in any given time period.

Q12. B

When the right paddle is being used, the paddle is pushing against water on the right-hand side of the canoe. This force pushes the canoe to the left.

Q13. 30 kg

$3 \div 1 = 3$

$90 \div 3 = 30$ kg

Q14. D

Points A, B, and C are all part of the same object. Therefore, one part cannot be making any more revolutions than another.

Q15. A

The 'claw' on a claw hammer is specifically used to remove nails.

Q16. B

Pliers have a part instilled within the tool that is specifically used for stripping the insulation on non-live electrical cables.

Q17. A

In order to tighten the bolt, you must turn it clockwise.

Q18. Z

Load Z has the greatest mechanical advantage.

Q19. B

When a pipe narrows, the same volume occupies a smaller space. For the same volume to pass points A and B in a given time, the speed must be greater at point B. As the circumference of the pipe gets smaller, the velocity will increase.

Q20. C

Water is denser than oil and will therefore sink to the bottom. The oil will remain on top.

Q21. A

The horizontal g-force of the truck's direction causes the pendulum to move towards the back of the truck.

Q22. 4 kg

The distance at point X from the pivot/balance point is five times that of the other side (10 metres vs. 2 metres). Therefore, the weight must be five times less than the 20kg weight to balance the beam.

Q23. 147 N

$60 \div 4 = 15$

$15 \times 9.8 = 147$

Q24. 4. They provide a wider field-of-view.

Convex mirrors, also know as fish-eye mirrors, are frequently used as rear-view wing mirrors in vehicles due to the wider field-of-view that they provide.

Q25. 30 psi

Pressure = Force / Area or P = F / A. Therefore, P = 60 / 2 = 30.

Mechanical Comprehension Test 2

Question 1. Both water buckets are filled to the top. Which water bucket most accurately demonstrates how water would leak from the bucket if 4 small holes were made on the side of the buckets?

X   Y

Question 2. Which rope is needed to support the load on the crane? Circle your answer.

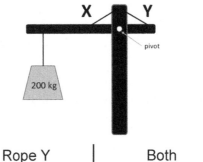

Rope X | Rope Y | Both | Neither

Question 3. Magdalena's bicycle has 14 teeth on the rear gear and 56 teeth on the front gear. Her bicycle is single-speed. If Magdalena pedaled her bicycle at 60 revolutions per minute (rpm), how fast would her rear wheel rotate?

Question 4. The two balls shown are of identical density. When rolled toward each other at the same speed, what will happen to ball A?

A. It will stop

B. It will roll over ball B

C. It will be propelled backward

D. It will keep moving forward

A   B

Question 5. An aircraft carrier is travelling due east at 0.8 m/s with a current flow of 0.2 m/s due east. After 1 hour of travelling, how far has the ship travelled in kilometers?

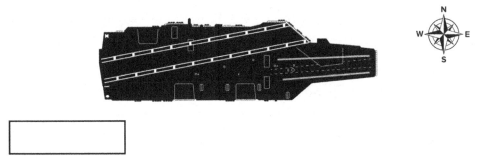

Question 6. If bulb 2 is removed, how many bulbs will illuminate?

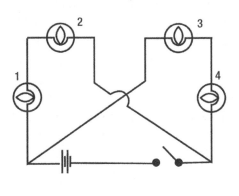

Question 7. When the switch is closed, how many bulbs will illuminate when bulb 3 is removed, and replaced with cable?

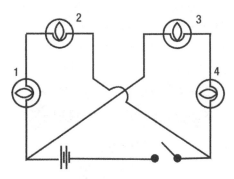

Question 8. The following three HGVs are parked on an incline. Their centre of gravity is identified by a dot. Which of the three HGVs is least likely to fall over?

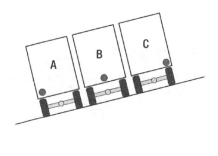

Question 9. Which of the following most resembles a lever? Circle your answer.

Swing | Car | Elevator | Seesaw

Question 10. A builder is told to pitch his ladder a third of the working height away from the building below. How many metres away from the building should the foot of the ladder be placed?

12 METRES

Question 11. A truck containing petrol is travelling at 40 mph in the direction of the large arrow. If it had to suddenly brake, which diagram best demonstrates what would happen to the petrol the truck is transporting at the time of braking suddenly?

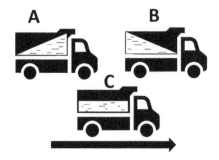

Question 12. Both wheel X and wheel Y both revolve at the same rate. If wheel X covers a linear distance of 18 ft, which of the following statements is true?

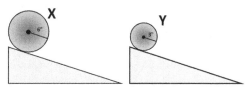

A. Wheel X will be half as quick as wheel Y to travel 18 ft

B. Wheel Y will be be twice as quick to travel 18 ft

C. Wheel Y will take 6 seconds to travel 18 ft

D. Wheel Y will take longer to travel 18 ft

Question 13. For the water to travel from Reservoir X to Reservoir Y and pass through filters 1 & 2, which valves need to be opened?

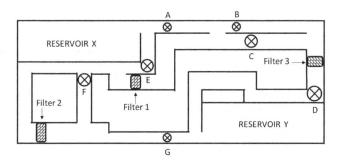

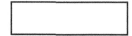

Question 14. If the wheel marked A rotates anti-clockwise, in which direction will the star marked B rotate?

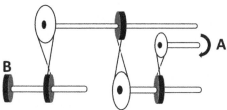

Question 15. Which option best defines what 'Energy' is?

A. The capacity to do work/change something

B. The application of force

C. Weight resistance

D. Motion

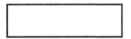

Question 16. A hot air balloon is able to float because:

A. The hot air is turbo-charged

B. The hot air is less dense than the external air

C. The hot air is denser than the external air

D. It is filled with helium

Question 17. Water is flowing into the following tank through the left-hand side inlet pipe at a rate of 18 litres per minute. If the water is flowing out through the lower right-hand side outlet pipe at a rate of 14 litres per minute, approximately how much time will it take for the tank to overflow?

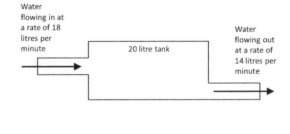

Question 18. If the wheel rotates anticlockwise, what will happen to X?

A. It will move to the right and stop.

B. It will move to the left and stop.

C. It will move left and right.

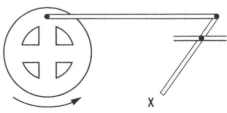

Question 19. How much force is required to lift the load?

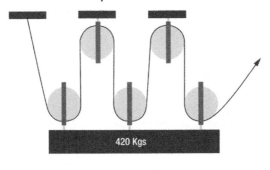

420 Kgs

Question 20. How much weight is required to hold the load?

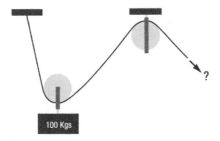

100 Kgs

?

Question 21. Which tool would you use for rounding the edges of metal pins and fasteners?

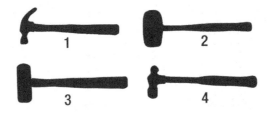

Question 22. A ship sails due West. Then, it changes its course as shown on the dotted line. Which direction is it now travelling in?

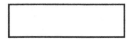

Question 23. Which of the following tools is best for taking exact measurements of two opposite points of an object? Circle your answer.

Depth Gauge | Caliper | Surface Level | Wire Gauge

Question 24. Which electrical component is the following a description of:

As light intensity increases, the resistance goes down.

Light emitting diode. | Variable resistor. | Thermistor. | Light dependent resistor.

Question 25. Which crane is working under the least tension?

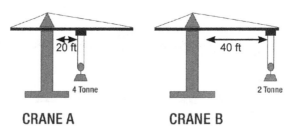

CRANE A   CRANE B

Answers to Mechanical Comprehension Test 2

Q1. Y

The water pressure is higher at lower points of the bucket, causing water streams to go further.

Q2. Rope X

Rope X acts against the force of gravity, preventing the crane arm from pivoting downwards. Rope Y is superfluous. Rope Y would not act against the force of gravity.

Q3. 240 rpm. One full turn of the pedals is equal to $56 \div 14 = 4$ revolutions. To work out the rpm for the real wheel you need to multiply the speed the rider pedals the bicycle at (60 rpm) by 4. 4×60 rpm = 240 rpm.

Q4. D. It will keep moving forward. As both balls have the same density and are moving at the same speed, the larger ball (ball A) must have more momentum. Therefore, it will knock ball B backward and keep moving forward.

Q5. 3.6 km. The ship's net forward velocity is 1 m/s (0.8 + 0.2). 1 hour equals 3,600 seconds. $1 \times 3,600 = 2,600$ metres or 3.6 km.

Q6. No bulbs would illuminate because the circuit, in its current state, is not working. This is due to the switch being open.

Q7. Three bulbs would illuminate.

This is because the circuit would be complete.

Q8. C

By drawing a vertical line straight down from the centre of gravity, only the line for HGV C shows stability. Therefore, this HGV is least likely to fall over.

Q9. A seesaw is the only option which utilises a form of leverage to function.

Q10. 4 metres

The working height is 12 metres. The foot of the ladder must be placed 4 metres away from the building. $(12 \div 3 = 4)$

Q11. A

Newton's First Law of motion states that an object will remain in the same state of motion until a force acts to change the motion. Therefore, in this example, the petrol tries to continue moving in the same direction as the truck was moving.

Q12. D. Wheel Y will take longer to travel 18 ft. As wheel Y is smaller than wheel X it has to make more revolutions to travel the same distance. Therefore wheel Y takes longer.

Q13. Valves A and G

Q14. Anti-clockwise

All of the wheels must rotate in the same direction as they are all linked together.

Q15. A

The capacity to do work/change something

Q16. B

The burner inside the hot air balloon heats up the air inside the balloon. Hotter air is less dense than colder air. This makes the internal air hotter than the external air, resulting in the hot air rising. As a result, this causes the entire balloon to rise.

Q17. 5 minutes

Water is flowing in at a rate of 18 litres per minute; however, because water is also leaving the tank at a rate of 14 litres per minute, this means that only 4 litres per minute is effectively filling the tank. If the tank has a capacity of 20 litres, then it will take 5 minutes for it to overflow.

Q18. C It will move left and right as the wheel rotates.

Q19. 70 kg. The load weighs 420 kg and there are a total of six sections of rope supporting it. In order to calculate the force required to lift the load, simply divide the weight by the number of ropes in order to reach your answer:

- $420 \div 6 = 70$ kg

Q20. 50 kg. In this scenario the weight is suspended by two pulleys. This means the weight is split equally between the two pulleys. If you want to hold the weight you only have to apply half the weight of the load.

- $100 \div 2 = 50$ kg.

Q21. 4

Ball Peen Hammers are used to shape metal.

Q22. South

South is the direction which is 90 degrees clockwise from West.

Q23. Caliper

Q24. Light dependent resistor.

Q25. Both the same

Mechanical Comprehension Test 3

Question 1. Out of the 3 labelled water tanks, which of them will overfill?

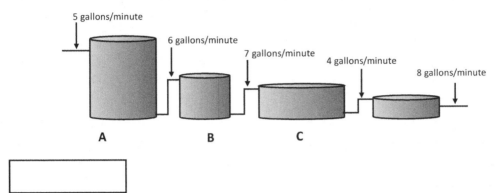

5 gallons/minute
6 gallons/minute
7 gallons/minute
4 gallons/minute
8 gallons/minute

A   B   C

Question 2. Cog Y has a radius of 14 inches, whereas cog X has a radius of 7 inches. If cog Y starts rotating anticlockwise at a constant 10 revolutions per minute (rpm), which one of the following statements will be true?

Cog X will make 10 clockwise rotations per minute

Cog X will make 2 clockwise rotations per minute

Cog X will make 10 anticlockwise rotations per minute

Cog X will make 20 clockwise rotations per minute

Y   X

Question 3. Which set of ice (both sets weigh 95 g) will cool a container of water quickest?

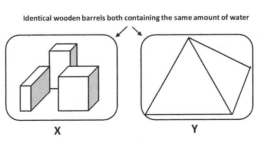

Identical wooden barrels both containing the same amount of water

X   Y

Question 4. All of the shapes shown are hollow and filled with water. If they are all the exact same weight, which one will be the hardest to push on its side?

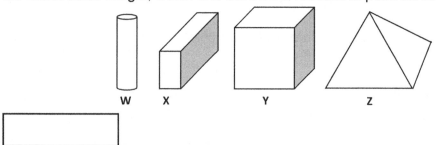

W   X   Y   Z

Question 5. If a 12 ft long ramp is 8 ft high, what is the ideal mechanical advantage of the plane?

Question 6. If the motor wheel rotates in a clockwise direction, what happens to B and C?

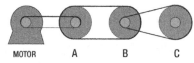

MOTOR   A   B   C

A. B and C will move clockwise.

B. B and C will move anti-clockwise.

C. B will move clockwise, and C will move anti-clockwise.

D. B will move anti-clockwise, and C will move clockwise.

Question 7. If Cog B turns clockwise, which of the other cogs will also turn clockwise?

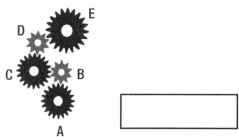

Question 8. At which point will the beam balance?

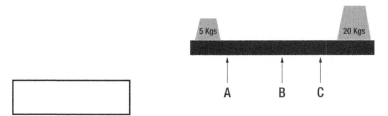

Question 9. If water is poured in at point D, which tube will overflow first?

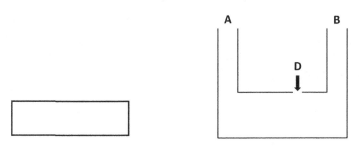

Question 10. Which pulley system will be the easiest to lift the bucket of water?

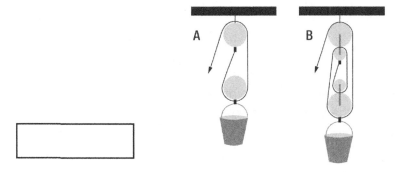

Question 11. How much weight in kg should be placed at the location of the question mark to balance the weights?

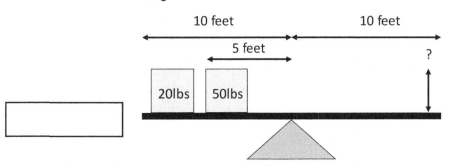

Question 12. What would happen to a balloon full of air, if you were to place it 15 feet below a water surface?

A. The volume of the balloon would increase.

B. The volume of the balloon would stay the same.

C. The balloon would explode.

D. The volume of the balloon would decrease.

Question 13. In the diagram, the spring can be stretched 1 inch by a force of 200 lbs. How much force needs to be applied to the object in order to move the object 4.5 inches to the left?

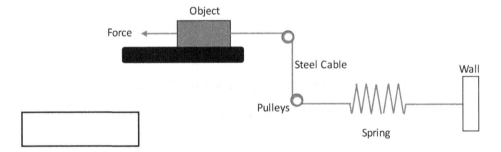

Question 14. If gear A in the diagram begins spinning clockwise, what will happen to the spring that is attached to the wall? Circle your answer.

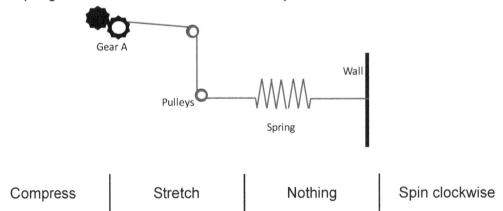

Compress | Stretch | Nothing | Spin clockwise

Question 15. What transfers from a carpet made from nylon to give off a static electrical shock? Circle your answer.

Nucleus	Protons	Electrons	Atoms

Question 16. When the handle makes a complete rotation, how far will the weight lower?

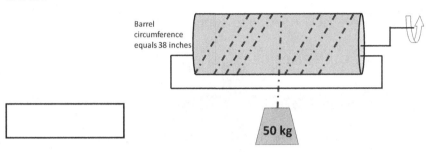

Barrel circumference equals 38 inches

50 kg

Question 17. A wooden disk with an integral metal disk inserted will stop in which position when rolled on a flat surface?

X   Y   Z

Question 18. A warship is travelling due north east at 1.2 m/s against a current flow of 0.6 m/s due south west. After 3 hours of travelling, how far has the ship travelled?

A. 6.48 km north east of its starting location

B. 1.8 km north east of its starting location

C. 1.8 km south west of its starting location

D. 64.8 km south west of its starting location

Question 19. A spring scale is used to measure newton weight. It is loaded with one 15-newton weight and the spring stretches to 0.6 centimetres. If it is loaded with another 15-newton weight, what is the deflection?

Question 20. Which rope(s) are NOT needed to support the crane's load?

Question 21. What type of gear should be applied if gear shafts are not aligned parallel to each other?

Coil Gear | Bevel Gear | Shift Gear | Ball Gear

Question 22. A hydraulic jack performs the task of moving an object by_____

A. Using spring compression

B. Pressurisation of gas and weights

C. Applying pressure to oil

D. A lever and locking system

Question 23. Where will the highest temperature change take place throughout 24 hours in the image below?

The Water | The Sand | No difference

Question 24. Which of the following is the measure of how much matter is in an object?

Density | Weight | Mass | Force

Question 25.

When throwing a ball, a person's arm is acting as a _____

First-class lever | Second-class lever | Third-class lever | None of the above

Answers to Mechanical Comprehension Test 3

Q1. C

Water tank C will overflow eventually as it has an inflow greater than its outflow.

Q2. D. Cog Y will make 20 clockwise rotations per minute.

Cog Y makes 10 revolutions per minute. Cog X is half the size of cog Y, therefore cog X will make double the revolutions per minute, 20 rpm (multiply the number of revolutions cog Y makes by the inverse of ½ which is $\frac{2}{1}$, $10 \times 2 = 20$).

Q3. X

The ice in Set X has a greater surface area.

Q4. Z

Shape Z has the widest base relative to its height.

Q5. 1.5.

The following formula is used to work out the mechanical advantage of an inclined plane: Mechanical Advantage = Distance Load Travels / Height Load Is Lifted

Therefore, $12 \div 8 = 1.5$.

Q6. A

B and C will move clockwise as the motor wheel moves clockwise.

Q7. Cog D is the only other cog which will rotate clockwise.

Cog B rotates clockwise, causing cog A and C to rotate anti-clockwise. Cog D rotates clockwise, causing cog E to rotate anti-clockwise.

Q8. C

In order to balance the beam the point of balance will move closer to the heavier weight – which in this case is the 20 kg weight.

Q9. Both

The entrance and exit points of the container are level, therefore, both will overflow at the same time.

Q10. Pulley B

Pulley A has a mechanical advantage of 2 whereas pulley B has a mechanical advantage of 4.

Q11. 45 lbs

f = (20 × 10) + (50 × 5) ÷ 10

f = (200) + (250) ÷ 10

f = 450 ÷ 10 = 45 lbs

Q12. D

If you were to place a balloon full of air 15 feet under a water surface, the volume of the balloon would decrease. According to Boyle's Law, the pressure on the balloon from the water would press inwards, and therefore it would cause the balloon to shrink in size and subsequently decrease the volume of the balloon.

Q13. 900 lbs

4.5 × 200 = 900 lbs

Q14. The spring will compress

If the gears moved in a clockwise manner, that means the cable connecting everything together is going to move right (towards the wall), and so the spring will be compressed.

Q15. Electrons

Electrons are transferred from a nylon carpet to give off a static electrical charge. Protons remain in the nucleus and cannot be transferred.

Q16. 38 inches.

One complete rotation of the winch will lower the weight 38 inches – the circumference of the barrel.

Q17. X

The metal disk is the heaviest part of the object, so it will cause the wooden disk to stop with the metal part at the bottom.

Q18. A. 6.48 km north east of its starting location.

The ship's net forward velocity is 0.6 m/s (1.2 − 0.6). 1 hour equals 3,600 seconds. 0.6 × 3600 = 2160 metres or 2.16 km distance travelled per hour. 2.16 × 3 = 6.48 km of distance travelled after 3 hours.

Q19. 1.2 cm

15 newtons = 0.6 cm

15 + 15 = 30 newtons

30 newtons = 1.2 cm

Q20. Ropes A & C

Rope B acts against the force of gravity, preventing the crane arm from pivoting downwards. Ropes A and C are superfluous as they do not act against the force of gravity.

Q21. Bevel Gear

A bevel gear is also known as an intersecting gear. Because the axes of the bevel gear intersect, it is ideal for fixing issues related to parallel gears.

Q22. C. By applying pressure to oil.

Hydraulic jacks work by putting pressure on a liquid. In this case, because oil cannot be compressed, when pressure is placed on the oil it will result in a lifting motion – thus the hydraulic jack is working as intended.

Q23. The Sand

Because sand is a better thermal conductor than water, the sand will heat faster. Water retains heat far longer than said, thus, sand is more prone to larger temperature changes than water.

Q24. Mass

Mass is the measure of 'the total amount' or 'matter' in an object.

Q25. A third class lever

A third class lever is when the force is in-between the load and the fulcrum. In this case, the person's arm applies force towards the direction that the ball is thrown, resulting in the ball travelling in that direction.

IQ

IQ Test 1

Question 1. What is two thirds of one half of three quarters of 800?

```
┌─────────────────────────────────┐
│                                 │
│                                 │
└─────────────────────────────────┘
```

Question 2. Which word below makes best sense when placed in the sentence? Circle your answer.

I practised all year so I would _____ the 200 metre sprint.

won | winning | win | winned

Question 3. Which 5-letter word can be placed at the beginning of the below words to create a new word?

bath   shed   shot   stream

```
┌─────────────────────────────────┐
│                                 │
│                                 │
└─────────────────────────────────┘
```

Question 4. Solve the anagram.

TLAEEITSL

```
┌─────────────────────────────────┐
│                                 │
│                                 │
└─────────────────────────────────┘
```

Question 5. Today is Friday, what day was two weeks before the day before yesterday?

```
┌─────────────────────────────────┐
│                                 │
│                                 │
└─────────────────────────────────┘
```

Question 6. Which of the below is the best translation of this proverb? Circle your answer.

It's no use locking the stable door after the horse has bolted.

A) You should use a lock with a bolt on stable doors.

B) It's too late taking precautions after damage has occurred.

C) Horses shouldn't be locked inside stables.

D) Bolts on stable doors are not effective.

Question 7. If the 5th day of the month is a Saturday, what day was the 1st?

Question 8. Meghan and Hashim are stood together. Meghan walks north for 12 metres, then east for 9 metres, then north for 3 metres. Hashim walks north for 6 metres, then west for 11 metres, then south for 15 metres.

Following the paths they each took, how far apart are Meghan and Hashim now?

Question 9. Rowan goes to the supermarket each week. On week one he spends £55.20. On week two he spends 20% more than week one. On week three he spends £6.30 less than week one. On week 4 he spends one quarter less than week 2.

How much has Rowan spent in total?

Question 10. To consent is to…

Circle your answer.

A) Arrange a date

B) Agree permission

C) Consider a request

D) Propose an idea

Question 11. Solve the anagram.

OETISRGTIRNA

Question 12. Which 3-letter word can be placed at the beginning of the below words to create a new word?

son   side   weed   food

Question 13. Which word below makes best sense when placed in the sentence? Circle your answer.

I _____ my exam results up because I was unhappy with my score.

teared | torn | tore | tear

Question 14. It takes Aiysha 30 minutes to walk 2 miles. How long will it take her to walk 15 miles?

Question 15. The season after winter is?

Question 16. To postulate is to...

Circle your answer.

A) Sit up straight

B) Move closer to someone

C) Pretend to be ill

D) Assume something is true

Question 17. Christian is re-roofing a house with slate tiles. The roof needs 14 rows of 35 tiles. Christian can buy roof tiles for £45 for a pack of 25. He has budgeted £1,000 for the roof tiles, how much of his budget will he have left over?

Question 18. Which word can be added to the end of MO and the beginning of ION to create two new words?

Question 19. Ola has 18 crayons. 5 are purple, one ninth are green, there are half as many blue as there are orange, there are three times as many orange as green. The remainder of her crayons are yellow.

3 crayons are yellow.   **TRUE**   **FALSE**

Question 20. Which is least like the others? Circle your answer.

Africa | Albania | Argentina | Austria

Question 21. Solve the anagram K R E O P E C O D W and you get a type of:

A) Food

B) Tool

C) Bird

D) Vehicle

Question 22. What is the 7ᵗʰ month of the year?

Question 23. Which of the below is not equal to 15^2? Circle your answer.

A) 315 – 90

B) $5^2 \times 9$

C) 30 + (65 ×3)

D) (565 ÷ 5) + (26 ÷ 2)

Question 24. Which of the below does **not** mean the same as:

Every Monday after school I go to football practice. On the way home I get fish and chips for dinner.

Circle your answer.

A) I get fish and chips every Monday after football practice.

B) I have football practice on Mondays. Afterwards I get fish and chips.

C) On Monday I have fish and chips then go to football practice.

D) I always have fish and chips on Monday after I've been to football practice.

Question 25. Noah likes apples but not bananas. He likes grapes but not carrots. He likes lemons but not oranges.

Does Noah like turnips?

Question 26. Eight years ago Frankie was half the age of Dominique. In five years' Dominique will be 19 years older than Frankie.

How old is Dominique now?

Question 27. Which of the below is not equal to $\sqrt{81} \times 3$. Circle your answer.

A) 100 − 73

B) 5 × 5 + 2

C) 4 × 7

D) 12% of 225

Question 28. Which of the below is the best translation of this proverb? Circle your answer.

Opportunity seldom knocks twice

A) What you do is more important than what you say.

B) Be patient and good things will happen.

C) A door with a bell is more effective than one without.

D) Take a chance when it comes, it may not come again.

Question 29. Which is least like the others? Circle your answer.

Carrot | Tomato | Broccoli | Cauliflower

Question 30. Which word can be added to the end of INT and the beginning of ANGER to create two new words?

```
┌─────────────────────────────┐
│                             │
│                             │
│                             │
└─────────────────────────────┘
```

Question 31. Which of the below does **not** mean the same as:

During the sale I got a 15% discount on my new coat. I saved £30.

Circle your answer.

A) My coat cost £170 because I purchased it during the sale.

B) My coat was on sale, I only had to pay 85%.

C) I paid £30 for my new coat, it was 15% off.

D) A 15% discount saved me £30 off the cost of my new coat.

Question 32. Mateo likes euros but not dollars. He likes kunas but not lempiras. He likes pounds but not pesos. Does he like kronas?

```
┌─────────────────────────────┐
│                             │
│                             │
│                             │
└─────────────────────────────┘
```

Question 33. Four hours ago it was nine hours until 7 pm. What time is it now?

```
┌─────────────────────────────┐
│                             │
│                             │
│                             │
└─────────────────────────────┘
```

Question 34. Heera is Pranjit's son's grandmother. Pranjit is Chhaya's daughter's uncle. Samaira is Neerav's cousin. Samaira is Heera's daughter's daughter. Chhaya is Samaira's brother's mother. If there are no other family members, what relation is Pranjit to Neerav?

```
┌─────────────────────────────┐
│                             │
│                             │
│                             │
└─────────────────────────────┘
```

Question 35. What is 20% of two thirds of 3 fifths of 650?

Question 36. In what month does the 16th week of the year begin?

Question 37. Which 5-letter word can be placed at the beginning of the below words to create a new word?

achieve   carriage   cover   ground

Question 38. Sophia travels at 45 mph for 1 hour and 40 minutes. How long will it take her to travel 120 miles?

Question 39. How much will it cost to tile this area?

£5.00

£2.50

£7.00

Question 40. Which word below makes best sense in the sentence? Circle your answer.

Elise was ready to _____ Olivia's apology for losing her car keys.

expect | except | accept | accepted

Question 41. Which word can be added to the end of UNC and the beginning of ICAL to create two new words?

Question 42. Which is closest in meaning to: PRECARIOUS

Circle your answer.

A) Valuable

B) Uncertain

C) Protected

D) Critical

Question 43. Which is least like the others? Circle your answer.

| Latte | Hot chocolate | Macchiato | Espresso |

Question 44. Solve the anagram.

LDACLCUETA

Question 45. In two hours, it will be 4 hours since it was 5 hours until 1 pm. What time is it now?

Answers to IQ Test 1

Q1. 200

Three quarters of 800 = 600

One half of 600 = 300

Two thirds of 300 = 200

Q2. win

Q3. Blood

Bloodbath, bloodshed, bloodshot, bloodstream

Q4. Satellite

Q5. Wednesday

Q6. B - It's too late taking precautions after damage has occurred.

Q7. Tuesday

Q8. 44 metres

Q9. £220.02

Q10. B - Agree permission

Q11. Registration

Q12. Sea

Q13. tore

Q14. 225 minutes (3 hours and 45 minutes)

Q15. Spring

Q16. D - Assume something is true

Q17. £100

The roof needs 490 tiles.

Christian will need 20 packs of tiles.

Q18. ON

Moon

Onion

Q19. False

Purple = 5

Green = 2

Blue = 3

Orange = 6

Yellow = 2

Q20. Africa

Africa is a continent, all the others are countries.

Q21. C - Bird

Woodpecker

Q22. July

Q23. D - (565 ÷ 5) + (26 ÷ 2)

(565 ÷ 5) + (26 ÷ 2) = 226

Q24. C - On Monday I have fish and chips then go to football practice.

Q25. No

Apples, grapes, and lemons have 6 letters.

Bananas, carrots, oranges and turnips have 7 letters.

Q26. 46 years old

The age gap between Dominique and Frankie will always be 19 years.

Therefore, if Dominique was twice the age of Frankie, Dominique would have to be 38.

Because the above was eight years ago, Dominique would have to be 46 years old.

Q27. C - 4 × 7

4 × 7 = 28

Q28. D - Take a chance when it comes, it may not come again.

Q29. Tomato

Tomatoes are a fruit, the rest are vegetables

Q30. END

Intend

Endanger.

Q31. C - I paid £30 for my new coat, it was 15% off.

Q32. Yes

Euros, kunas, pounds, and kronas are currencies used within Europe.
Dollars, lempiras, and pesos are currencies used within America.

Q33. 2 pm

Q34. Father

Pranjit is Neerav's father.

Q35. 52
Three fifths of 650 = 390
Two thirds of 390 = 260
20% of 260 = 52

Q36. April

Q37. Under

Underachieve, undercarriage, undercover, underground

Q38. 2 hours and 40 minutes

Q39. £334
$50 \times 5 = 250$
$14 \times 2.5 = 35$
$7 \times 7 = 49$

Q40. accept

Q41. LOG

Unclog

Logical

Q42. B - Uncertain

Q43. Hot chocolate

The others are types of coffee.

Q44. Calculated

Q45. 10 am

IQ Test 2

Question 1. Which of these two words are closest in meaning? Circle your answer.

angry | kind | innate | intimate | indignant | calm

Question 2. Which of these two words are closest in meaning? Circle your answer.

bold | marble | brave | entire | partial | between

Question 3. Which of these two words are closest in meaning? Circle your answer.

throw | move | climb | hurl | warp | dial

Question 4. Which of these two words are closest in meaning? Circle your answer.

group | pile | blast | fly | gale | soar

Question 5. Which of these two words are closest in meaning? Circle your answer.

guarantee | build | destroy | track | create | dismiss

Question 6. What number completes the following sequence?

5, 9, 14, 20, 27, 35, **?**

Question 7. What number completes the following sequence?

10, 15, 25, 30, 40, 45, **?**

Question 8. What number completes the following sequence?

4, 5, 10, 11, 22, 23, 46, 47, **?**

Question 9. What number completes the following sequence?

7, 14, 21, 28, 35, 42, **?**

Question 10. What number completes the following sequence?

6, 18, 20, 60, 62, 186, **?**

Question 11. What is 120% of 30 added to 40% of 20?

Question 12. Divide 712 by 4 and add 28. What is the answer?

Question 13. What is the missing digit?

6?5 + 76 = 741

Question 14. What is 320 divided in a ratio of 6:2?

```
┌─────────────────────────────┐
│                             │
│                             │
│                             │
└─────────────────────────────┘
```

Question 15. What is 75% expressed as a decimal?

```
┌─────────────────────────────┐
│                             │
│                             │
│                             │
└─────────────────────────────┘
```

Question 16. Which of the following is the odd one out? Circle your answer.

denim | steel | cotton | wool | leather

Question 17. Which of the following two words are the most opposite in meaning? Circle your answer.

greed | gluttony | apathy | generosity | courage | careless

Question 18. Which of the following two words are closest in meaning? Circle your answer.

break | contain | eviscerate | propose | enclose | brighten

Question 19. Persist is to surrender as confirm is to ? Circle your answer.

deny | suppose | decry | beware | arrive

Question 20. Which of the words in the brackets is most similar in meaning to the word outside of the brackets? Circle your answer.

ASCERTAIN (establish | suppose | imply | govern | expedite)

Question 21. Which of the following sentences is most grammatically correct and free from spelling errors?

a) She went to the shops, to bought a carton of milk.

b) She went to the shops to buy a carton of milk.

c) She go to the shops to buy a carton of milk.

d) She go too the shops to buy a carton of milk.

e) She went to the shops but bought a carton of milk.

```
┌─────────────────────────────────┐
│                                 │
│                                 │
└─────────────────────────────────┘
```

Question 22. What number completes the sequence?

6, 18, 20, **?**, 62

```
┌─────────────────────────────────┐
│                                 │
│                                 │
└─────────────────────────────────┘
```

Question 23. It takes 12 people 30 hours to dig up a road. How many hours would it take 15 people to dig up a road?

```
┌─────────────────────────────────┐
│                                 │
│                                 │
└─────────────────────────────────┘
```

Question 24. What number completes the sequence?

10, 14, 15, 19, **?**, 24

```
┌─────────────────────────────────┐
│                                 │
│                                 │
└─────────────────────────────────┘
```

Question 25. Series is to pilot as album is to ? Circle your answer.

beginning | debut | finale | conclusion

Question 26. What is the missing digit?

$298 - 10? = 197$

Question 27. What is 30% of 190 added to 70% of 600?

Question 28. It takes 20 people 14 hours to build a house. How long does it take for 35 people to build a house?

Question 29. What number completes the sequence?

10, 8, 13, 11, 16, 14, ?

Question 30. Which of the following sentences is grammatically correct?

a) There was no way that he was going too made it back home in time.

b) There was no way what he was going to make it back home in time.

c) There were no way that he was going to make it back home in time.

d) There was no way that he was going to make it back home in time.

e) There were no ways that he wasn't going to make it back home in time.

Question 31. Which is the odd one out? Tick your answer.

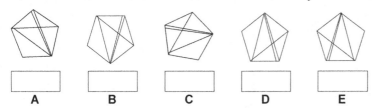

A	B	C	D	E

Question 32. Which is the odd one out? Tick your answer.

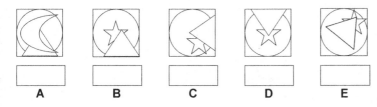

A	B	C	D	E

Question 33. Which is the odd one out? Tick your answer.

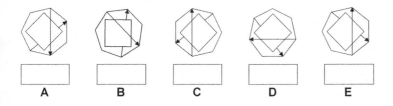

A	B	C	D	E

Question 34. Which is the odd one out? Tick your answer.

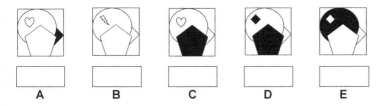

A	B	C	D	E

Question 35. Which is the odd one out? Tick your answer.

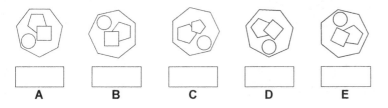

A	B	C	D	E

Question 36. What comes next in the sequence? Tick your answer.

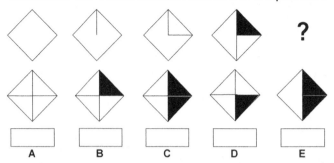

A	B	C	D	E

Question 37. What comes next in the sequence? Tick your answer.

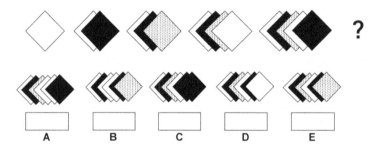

A	B	C	D	E

Question 38. What comes next in the sequence? Tick your answer.

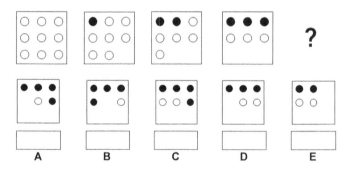

A	B	C	D	E

Question 39. What comes next in the sequence? Tick your answer.

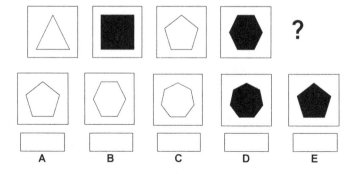

A	B	C	D	E

Question 40. What comes next in the sequence? Tick your answer.

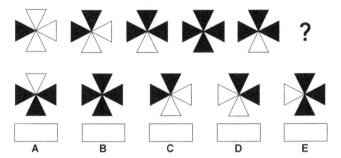

?

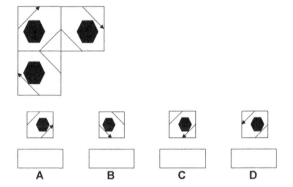

| A | B | C | D | E |

Question 41. Which of the tiles below completes the pattern? Tick your answer.

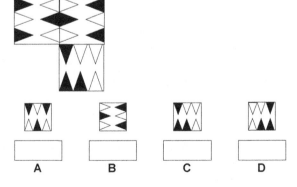

| A | B | C | D |

Question 42. Which of the tiles below completes the pattern? Tick your answer.

| A | B | C | D |

Question 43

Which of the tiles below completes the pattern? Tick your answer.

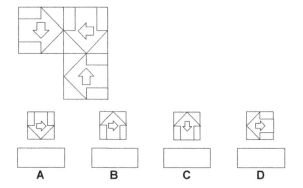

Question 44

Which of the tiles below completes the pattern? Tick your answer.

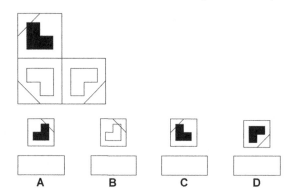

Question 45

Which of the tiles below completes the pattern? Tick your answer.

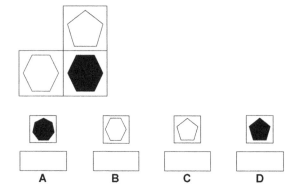

Answers to IQ Test 2

Q1. angry, indignant

'Angry' and 'Indignant' are synonyms.

Q2. bold, brave

'Bold' and 'Brave' are synonyms.

Q3. throw, hurl

'Throw' and 'Hurl' are synonyms.

Q4. fly, soar

'Fly' and 'Soar' are synonyms.

Q5. build, create

'Build' and 'Create' are synonyms.

Q6. 44

The number added increases by 1 each time (+4, +5, +6, +7, +8, +9, and so on).

Q7. 55

Alternate between +5 and +10 (+5, +10, +5, +10, and so on).

Q8. 94

Alternate between adding 1 and doubling the previous number (+1, ×2, +1, ×2, +1, ×2, and so on).

Q9. 49

Add 7 to the previous number to get the next number.

Q10. 188

Alternate between adding 2 and multiplying by 3 (+2, ×3, +2, ×3, +2, ×3, and so on).

Q11. 44

120% of 30 is 36. 40% of 20 is 8. 36 + 8 = 44.

Q12. 206.

712 ÷ 4 = 178. 178 + 28 = 206.

Q13. 6

665 + 76 = 741.

Q14. 240:80

Divide 320 by 8 to get 40. Multiply 40 by 6 to get 240. Multiply 40 by 2 to get 80.

Q15. 0.75

100% is equal to 1. Therefore, 75% is equal to 0.75.

Q16. steel

denim, cotton, wool, and leather are all materials associated with clothing. Steel is not.

Q17. greed, generosity.

'Greed' means to hoard or take something for oneself. 'Generosity' means to give things to others.

Q18. contain, enclose

Both 'contain' and 'enclose' refer to the act of holding something, and keeping it in a confined space.

Q19. deny

'Surrender' is the opposite of 'persist'. 'Deny' is the opposite of 'confirm'.

Q20. establish

'Ascertain' means to make sure of something. The meaning of 'establish' is to find out something for certain. This means that these two words are closest in meaning.

Q21. b) She went to the shops to buy a carton of milk.

All of the other sentences contain some kind of grammatical error.

Q22. 60

Multiply by 3, then add 2 (×3, +2, ×3, +2, and so on). 20 × 3 = 60.

Q23. 24

It takes 360 person hours to dig up the road (12 × 30 = 360). To find out how long it would take 15 people, divide 360 by 15 to get 24 hours.

Q24. 20

Add 4, then add 1 (+4, +1, +4, and so on). 19 + 1 = 20.

Q25. debut

The 'pilot' episode of a television series or programme is the first episode. A debut album is an artist's first album.

Q26. 1

Explanation 298 − 101 = 197

Q27. 477

30% of 190 is 57 (190 ÷ 10 × 3 = 57). 70% of 600 is 420 (600 ÷ 10 × 7 = 420). 57 + 420 = 477.

Q28. 8

It takes 280 person hours to build the house (20 × 14 = 280). Therefore, it takes 8 hours for 14 people to build a house (280 ÷ 35 = 8).

Q29. 19

Minus 2, add 5 (−2, +5, −2, +5, and so on). 14 + 5 = 19.

Q30. d) There was no way that he was going to make it back home in time.

All of the other sentences have some kind of grammatical error.

Q31. D

A, B, C, and E are all rotations of each other. D is a reflection.

Q32. A

B, C, D, and E all contain a star shape. A does not.

Q33. E

A, B, C, and D are rotations. E is a reflection.

Q34. B

A, C, D, and E all contain a black shape. B does not.

Q35. C

A, B, D, and E all contain a square shape. C does not.

Q36. C

A straight line is added to each corner of the diamond. Once this creates a triangle shape, the triangle is filled in on the next step.

Q37. E

A diamond is added in the following order: white, black, then dotted.

Q38. A

From the top-left corner, a dot turns from white to black each step. From the bottom-right, a dot disappears each step.

Q39. C

The shape gets one extra side each step in the sequence. It alternates between black and white.

Q40. D

The triangles change from white to black in a clockwise rotation, then black to white in a clockwise rotation.

Q41. C

The top left square and top right square are mirrored, with the direction of the arrow being flipped. Therefore, the bottom-left image must be mirrored by the bottom-right, with the arrow flipped. This makes option C the correct answer.

Q42. D

The top-left and top-right squares are mirrored. Therefore, the bottom-left square must mirror the bottom-right. This means D is the correct answer.

Q43. B

Moving clockwise between the four squares, the big arrow rotates 90 degrees clockwise in each square. The small arrow also rotates 90 degrees clockwise in each square.

Q44. A

The bottom two squares are mirrored. Therefore, the top-right square must mirror the top-left square. This makes A the correct answer.

Q45. D

The bottom two squares contain the same shape (a hexagon), but the colour is inverted from white to black. This means that the top-left shape must be a black pentagon to match the shape on the top-right. This makes D the correct answer.

Personality Tests

Personality Tests allow employers to assess a person's suitability for a job role, through an extensive examination of the candidate's personality traits.

Personality has become an increasingly reliable method of assessing whether a candidate is suitable for a job. By utilising these simple tests, employers are able to narrow down their choices based on desired personality traits. Personality traits represent different tendencies and preferences, rather than exact predictors of behaviour. These tests are designed to assess your individual and interpersonal behavioural qualities, which can then be examined against the needs of the job role.

Employers will most likely use one of four main personality tests, to assess a person's characteristics. However, all of the tests are designed in a similar manner, and are influenced by 'The Big 5' model of personality. This is a behavioural model which argues that every human being can be understood and analysed through five main personality traits: neuroticism, agreeableness, openness, extroversion, and conscientiousness. This is often referred to as the NEO-PI test.

This chapter will give you the opportunity to answer sample tests, which will then be analysed in order to give you a broad idea of your personality.

Neuroticism

5: Agree

4: Mostly Agree

3: Neither Agree or Disagree

2: Mostly Disagree

1: Disagree

Question	5	4	3	2	1
1. After a meeting, I mull things over.					
2. I worry about important meetings.					
3. I spend a lot of time feeling fearful, for no apparent reason.					
4. If I sense people don't like me, I often get offended.					
5. I have a tendency to take things personally.					
6. People are generally too touchy and emotional.					
7. I always keep my feelings to myself.					
8. I rarely act upon impulse.					
9. I rarely get frustrated with difficult people.					
10. I often idealise others.					
11. I get very paranoid when I am on my own.					
12. I doubt myself a lot.					
13. I think about myself a lot.					
14. I don't take pride in my appearance.					
15. I tend to withdraw from large crowds.					

Scoring for Neuroticism

Now that you've answered the questions regarding neuroticism, we can evaluate your scores. As you can see, each answer option has a score from 1 to 5 (Agree = 5, Mostly Agree = 4, and so on). We can use this to evaluate the levels of neuroticism in your personality. See the table below to find out your results and explanations for each.

Low: 15-34	If you scored between these figures, you have a low level of neuroticism. This means that you are less likely to feel upset or anxious, and are less emotionally reactive. In other words, you are more emotionally stable and demonstrate a high level of calmness, rationale, and capability towards dealing with your emotions. Whilst being emotionally stable is an advantage, you do not want to come across as a person who is not interested in their work. You need to be able to show some passion and enthusiasm. A low score suggests a person who is relatively free from negative feelings; they are able to keep their feelings under control, and don't let their personal life interfere with their work life.
Medium: 35-54	You often appear in control of your emotions. You tend to keep your feelings bottled up the best you can, and try not to let personal problems get in the way of your work. However, most people are prone to the occasional setback or upset. You may experience sadness and emotional turmoil occasionally, but you try to limit how much of it you show whilst at work. Whilst you may show some levels of vulnerability, you come across as a strong, independent and capable person, who tends to not let their feelings interfere with their work.
High: 55-75	A high level of neuroticism means that you experience more than one of the attributes explored throughout the chapter (i.e. anxiety, hostility, depression, etc). People who score highly are often emotionally reactive. This means that you are extremely sensitive and volatile, demonstrating emotional instability. You tend to feel inferior to others; you often feel awkward, shy, nervous, and vulnerable in social situations, and find it difficult to be yourself. A high level of neuroticism can often affect a person's way of thinking, their behaviour, and their feelings. Quite often, a person with high levels of neuroticism feels hopeless and frustrated with themselves, and often takes it out on others.

Agreeableness

5: Agree
4: Mostly Agree
3: Neither Agree or Disagree
2: Mostly Disagree
1: Disagree

Question	5	4	3	2	1
1. I usually believe what people tell me.					
2. I am always honest.					
3. I consider myself a reliable and trustworthy person.					
4. I try not to correct people if they are mistaken.					
5. I am rarely direct with the people around me.					
6. I don't always say what I think.					
7. Compliments embarass me.					
8. I try not to boast about myself.					
9. I don't like being the centre of attention.					
10. I dislike confrontation.					
11. I am willing to help others.					
12. I follow the rules.					
13. I often change my behaviour to avoid upsetting people.					
14. I work best if I work in a team.					
15. Our fate is in our own hands.					

Scoring for Agreeableness.

Now that you've answered the questions regarding agreeableness, we can evaluate your scores. As you can see, each answer option has a score from 1 to 5 (Agree = 5, Mostly Agree = 4, and so on). We can use this to evaluate the levels of agreeableness in your personality. See the table below to find out your results and explanations for each.

Low: 15-34	Low scorers are often sceptical and suspicious about other people. You tend to be unfriendly and withdrawn from social situations, due to lack of trust and reliance on other people. You are assertive and demanding. You like to voice your opinions, and make sure your voice is heard. You are not afraid to confront other people, and you are not afraid of creating confrontation or dispute. You tend to be quite shrewd and perceptive. People who scored low often find it easier to work independently as opposed to working in a team. You don't like to interact or engage with other people, and find it difficult to trust and empathise with them.
Medium: 35-54	Overall, you are a kind-hearted, warm, and sympathetic person who generally gets along with most people. Although you may find it difficult to like everyone, you often take behavioural disagreements in your stride, and don't let them affect you. You are considered an agreeable person. You follow the rules, you get along with people, and you tend to take instruction well. However, sometimes you like to voice your opinion and therefore cause some level of disagreeable-ness. Employers like to see that people are able to disagree with something if the situation requires it, just as long as said people are not too controversial.
High: 55-75	You are the type of person who carries the traits of sympathy and cooperation. You are considered friendly, empathetic, and generally kind-hearted. You are a trusting person, who finds it easy to get along with people. However, you may also be someone who struggles to deal with confrontation, often because you're holding people to the same high standards that you yourself set. This leads to you not being assertive, or expressing how you really feel. In some careers, this could be considered a weakness; despite it only being down to your good nature. People with high levels of agreeableness have an optimistic view of human nature, and therefore believe strongly in the values of honesty, decency and trustworthiness. Just don't be too quick to assume the same about others – because unfortunately not everyone shares these same traits.

Extroversion

5: Agree
4: Mostly Agree
3: Neither Agree or Disagree
2: Mostly Disagree
1: Disagree

Question	5	4	3	2	1
1. I make friends easily.					
2. I like going to social events.					
3. I am easy to get to know as a person.					
4. I enjoy being in the company of others.					
5. I often find myself surrounded by lots of people.					
6. I hate being on my own.					
7. I voice my opinions.					
8. I am good at leading people.					
9. I find it easy to say what I want.					
10. I am not a cautious person.					
11. I am a thrill-seeker.					
12. I have previously put my career in jeopardy.					
13. I have a positive attitude towards life.					
14. I look for the best in people.					
15. I generally anticipate for the best possible outcome.					

Scoring for Extroversion

Now that you've answered the questions regarding extroversion, we can evaluate your scores. As you can see, each answer option has a score from 1 to 5 (Agree = 5, Mostly Agree = 4, and so on). We can use this to evaluate the levels of extroversion in your personality. See the table below to find out your results and explanations for each.

Low: 15-34	People who receive a low score overall on extroversion, are more introverted as opposed to extroverted. You are very reserved. You like to remain independent and you enjoy being on your own. Introverts are often described as shy, reserved, and aloof. You tend to withdraw from large crowds and prefer being distant and independent. People who score low in regards to extroversion are better suited to jobs that don't require much social interaction. So, a career that requires lots of face-to-face communication might not suit you
Medium: 35-54	If you scored medium on the scale, you are somewhere between introverted and extroverted. Although you are somewhat reserved when it comes to the people around you, you are able to make yourself approachable and friendly when necessary. Even though you might sometimes show characteristics like shyness, you also come across as sociable and outgoing. Employers like to see people who can not only show friendliness, compassion, and social awareness, but also people who are able to work on their own initiative, without having to rely on others.
High: 55-75	Having high levels of extroversion shows that you are a sociable person, who enjoys the company of other people. You show traits such as friendliness and warmth, and have a genuine interest in getting to know other people. You are dynamic, outgoing, and active, and seek companionship and social interaction. Extroverts don't often like being on their own, and consequently gravitate towards other people. Employers like to see people who are motivated, enthusiastic, and optimistic, so extroversion can be a really positive thing.

Conscientiousness

5: Agree

4: Mostly Agree

3: Neither Agree or Disagree

2: Mostly Disagree

1: Disagree

Question	5	4	3	2	1
1. I rarely misjudge a situation.					
2. I always feel confident.					
3. All of my work is proficient.					
4. I like structure.					
5. I like routine.					
6. I rarely lose my keys, phone, or other small belongings.					
7. I comply with rules and regulations in the workplace.					
8. I like to get things done.					
9. I do my work without questioning it.					
10. I have a lot of willpower.					
11. I am always an efficient worker.					
12. I am not easily distracted.					
13. I think before I act.					
14. I tend not to rush into things.					
15. I find it difficult not to overthink things.					

Scoring for Conscientiousness

Now that you've answered the questions regarding conscientiousness, we can evaluate your scores. As you can see, each answer option has a score from 1 to 5 (Agree = 5, Mostly Agree = 4, and so on). We can use this to evaluate the levels of conscientiousness in your personality. See the table below to find out your results and explanations for each.

Low: 15-34	If you scored low on conscientiousness, then this means that you are likely to be struggling for direction or motivation. People with low conscientiousness often haven't found the right role for them, or are uncertain about where to go next. This manifests in work ethic, where not knowing what you want to achieve, or how to achieve it, could be misconstrued as a lack of enthusiasm or care. The good news is, this trait is the easiest to improve! There are lots of tips out there on how to become more mindful and more self-aware – improving yourself is the first step to finding a career that's perfect for you!
Medium: 35-54	If you scored average on conscientiousness, then it is likely that are you someone who strives for achievement or success, but without thinking about it too much. You are an ambitious person, but succeeding professionally is not the be all and end all. People who score average on this scale are often hard workers, who value their career, without taking things too seriously. Sometimes you might show a lack of motivation, but once you get going you put your best efforts into your work, to achieve success.
High: 55-75	If you scored highly on this test, then it is likely that you are an ambitious person, who works hard to achieve your goals, both professionally and personally. You do your utmost to provide great quality work, and are not put off by the thought of challenge and hard work. Your career is your top priority. You value your profession and have goals for the future. Employers value people who show ambition and dedication to their job. Generally, having ambition reinforces your interest and motivation for your chosen career, which is always a positive thing for employers.

Openness

5: Agree
4: Mostly Agree
3: Neither Agree or Disagree
2: Mostly Disagree
1: Disagree

Question	5	4	3	2	1
1. I am preoccupied with arts or fiction.					
2. I welcome change.					
3. I am more interested in fantasy than facts.					
4. I enjoy the finer details in life.					
5. I enjoy taking walks in the countryside.					
6. I appreciate a good painting.					
7. I consider myself to be an open person.					
8. I get caught up in my emotions.					
9. I often feel emotionally vulnerable.					
10. I like to experience new things.					
11. I go with the flow; I don't really have a routine.					
12. I like to experiment.					
13. I often consume difficult reading material.					
14. I try to use a wide vocabulary.					
15. If something was unclear, I would conduct some research.					

Scoring for Openness

Now that you've answered the questions regarding openness, we can evaluate your scores. As you can see, each answer option has a score from 1 to 5 (Agree = 5, Mostly Agree = 4, and so on). We can use this to evaluate the levels of conscientiousness in your personality. See the table below to find out your results and explanations for each.

Low: 15-34	Those who score low on openness are extremely conventional. You rarely stray from the rules and regulations that are set, and therefore are not predisposed to challenge authority. You like to be assured of security and stability. You believe it is important to have a realistic understanding of the world we live in, and therefore have a clear and direct mindset. You don't fantasise or indulge in 'what ifs?'. You like routine and structure. You tend to keep your feelings and beliefs very close to your chest. You don't like to feel vulnerable by expressing yourself, so you tend to be more withdrawn. You know what you want, and you know exactly how to get it. You do what it takes to achieve your goals without deviating from convention.
Medium: 35-54	You are the type of person who not only likes taking adventures and experiencing new things, but you also like to feel secure and stable through routine and structure. You have ideas and values that you like to express. Although you can conform to the rules and regulations set by the company, you are not afraid to voice your opinion and stand up for yourself. Despite this, you are someone who generally voices their opinions in a constructive manner, without causing harm or hostility in the workplace environment.
High: 55-75	Individuals that possess a high level of openness show willingness to try different life experiences. They like experiencing different things and acknowledge the smaller things in life. You are considered imaginative. Your imagination tends to run wild and paint up vivid scenarios. This demonstrates that you have a creative and artistic ability, and enjoy interests such as art, nature and socialising. You are the type of person who is full of life, and are adventurous. You are full of ideas, and certain values are very important to you. High scorers for openness often challenge authority and tradition. They like to be able to put their mark on an important subject. They like to be able to voice their opinions.

A Few Final Words

You have now reached the end of your Psychometric testing guide. We have no doubt that you will feel more competent in a variety of different testing formats. We hope you have found this guide an invaluable insight into the different types of psychometric testing that you could face during job selection processes.

For any psychometric test, there are a few things to remember to help you perform at your best...

REMEMBER – THE THREE P'S!

1. Preparation. This may seem relatively obvious, but you will be surprised by how many people fail psychometric testing because they lacked preparation and knowledge regarding their test. You want to do your utmost to ensure the best possible chance of succeeding. Be sure to conduct as much preparation prior to your assessment, to ensure you are 100% prepared to complete the test successfully. Not only will practising guarantee improved scores, but it will also take some of the pressure off leading up to that all important test. Like anything, the more you practice, the more likely you are to succeed.

2. Perseverance. Everybody comes across times whereby they are set back or find obstacles in the way of their goals. The important thing to remember when this happens, is to use those setbacks and obstacles as a way of progressing. If you fail at something, consider 'why' you have failed. This will allow you to improve and enhance your performance for next time.

3. Performance. Your performance will determine whether or not you are likely to succeed. Attributes that are often associated with performance are self-belief, motivation and commitment. Self-belief is important for anything you do in life. It allows you to recognise your own abilities and skills and believe that you can do well. Believing that you can do well is half the battle! Being fully motivated and committed is often difficult for some people, but we can assure you that, nothing is gained without hard work and determination. If you want to succeed, you will need to put in that extra time and hard work.

Work hard, stay focused, and be what you want!

Good luck with your psychometric tests. We wish you the best of luck with all your future endeavours!

The how2become team

The How2Become team

Want more help?

Check out our other testing workbooks!

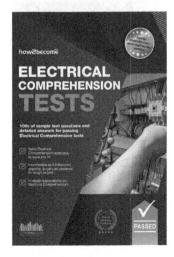

Get Access To
FREE
Reasoning
Test Questions

www.MyPsychometricTests.co.uk

Made in the USA
Coppell, TX
22 February 2020